this Book will Change you

You don't need more advice, you need a reset
where loneliness becomes your friend and overthinking finally finds pea

A BOOK BY
YOGESH DHIMAN

AF518987

BlueRoseONE.com
Stories Matter
NewDelhi • London

BLUEROSE PUBLISHERS
India | U.K.

For permissions requests or inquiries regarding this publication, please contact:

BLUEROSE PUBLISHERS
www.BlueRoseONE.com
info@bluerosepublishers.com
+91 8882 898 898
+4407342408967

ISBN: 978-93-7310-709-7

Cover Design: Daksh
Typesetting: Sagar

First Edition: October 2025

You don't need more advice.
You need a reset.

Yogesh Dhiman

"Healing is like planting seeds in a storm. You may not see the bloom right away, but every act of care, every moment of rest, every boundary you set is a root growing deeper. One day, you'll look back and realize, you didn't just survive. You grew."

Yogesh Dhiman

Contents

Part One

When It Feels Heavy

Chapter 1
The Weight of Waking Up

"It takes courage... to endure the sharp pains of self-discovery rather than choose to take the dull pain of unconsciousness that would last the rest of our lives."

Marianne Williamson

There are mornings when waking up feels like lifting a mountain. The alarm rings, but your body doesn't respond. Your mind is already racing, not with excitement, but with dread. The day ahead feels like a burden, not a promise. You lie there, staring at the ceiling, wondering how you'll make it through another day that looks just like the last–gray, heavy, and hollow. This feeling isn't laziness. It's the weight of emotional exhaustion. It's the residue of sleepless nights filled with worry, of days spent pretending to be okay. It's the loneliness that creeps in even when you're surrounded by people. It's the stress of responsibilities that feel too big and the negativity that whispers, "You're not enough."

Real-Life Examples:

A working mother, juggling her job and her children, wakes up already overwhelmed. She's been up late finishing reports and wakes early to pack lunches. Her body aches, her mind races, and she wonders if she'll ever feel rested again.

A college student, battling anxiety and isolation, wakes up in a dorm room that feels more like a cage than a home. The thought of attending class, interacting with peers, or even eating breakfast feels unbearable.

A retiree, living alone after the loss of a spouse, wakes up to silence. The house is quiet, the calendar is empty, and the loneliness is deafening.

These are not rare stories. They are everyday realities for millions. And yet, they often go unseen, unheard, and unspoken.

A Principle to Rise: The Principle of Gentle Momentum

When the weight of waking up feels too heavy, the solution isn't to force yourself into action. It's to start small and build gently. This is the Principle of Gentle Momentum.

Gentle Momentum means:

Start with one small win: Make your bed. Drink a glass of water. Open the curtains. These are not trivial–they are signals to your brain that the day has begun and you are participating in it.

Avoid overwhelming decisions early: Delay big choices until your mind has warmed up. Begin with routine, not responsibility.

Use movement to shift mood: A short walk, a stretch, or even standing up and breathing deeply can begin to lift the fog.

Speak kindly to yourself: Replace "I have to" with "I get to." Instead of "I'm failing," say "I'm trying." Your inner dialogue sets the tone for your day.

Connect, even briefly: A message to a friend, a smile at a neighbor, or a journal entry can remind you that you're not alone.

Gentle momentum doesn't solve everything, but it creates space for healing. It turns the act of waking up from a burden into a beginning. It honors your pain without letting it define your day.

Chapter 2
Anxiety That Won't Quit

"Everyone experiences a version of anxiety... To be a sensitive person that cares a lot is actually part of what makes you amazing."

Emma Stone

Anxiety doesn't always arrive with a warning. Sometimes, it's not a panic attack or a racing heart. Sometimes, it's just... always there. A quiet hum in the background of your thoughts. A constant tension in your chest. A feeling that something is wrong, even when everything seems fine.

This kind of anxiety doesn't shout–it whispers. It doesn't paralyze you, but it wears you down. It's the kind that lingers through your morning coffee, follows you into meetings, and curls up beside you at night. It's the kind that doesn't quit.

How It Feels

Persistent anxiety feels like:

Overthinking everything–from what you said in a conversation to what might go wrong tomorrow.

A tight chest or shallow breathing, even when you're sitting still.

Restlessness—you can't relax, even when you're exhausted.

Irritability—small things feel overwhelming, and you don't know why.

A sense of dread—like something bad is about to happen, even if there's no reason.

It's waking up already tired. It's checking your phone compulsively. It's needing constant reassurance. It's feeling like you're always "on," even when you're trying to rest.

Real-Life Examples

A young professional checks her email every few minutes, afraid she's missed something important. Even after work hours, her mind replays conversations with her boss, wondering if she sounded competent enough.

A father of two lies awake at night, worrying about bills, his children's future, and whether he's doing enough. He doesn't talk about it—he just carries it.

A student feels a constant pressure to perform. Even after submitting an assignment, they worry it wasn't good enough. They can't enjoy their free time because guilt and fear fill the silence.

This kind of anxiety is invisible. It doesn't always look like panic. It often looks like high-functioning stress, perfectionism, or just being "on edge." But it's real. And it's exhausting.

A Principle to Rise: The Principle of Grounding in the Present

When anxiety won't quit, the mind is often stuck in the future—imagining worst-case scenarios, replaying what-ifs, and trying to control the uncontrollable. The antidote is not to fight those thoughts, but to anchor yourself in the present. This is the Principle of Grounding in the Present.

Grounding in the Present means:

Name what's real right now: Say out loud or write down what you see, hear, feel, and know to be true in this moment. "I'm sitting on a chair. The room is quiet. I am safe."

Breathe with intention: Try the 4-7-8 method—inhale for 4 seconds, hold for 7, exhale for 8. It slows your nervous system and brings you back to your body.

Limit future forecasting: When your mind spirals into "what if," gently bring it back with "what is." Ask: "Is this happening now?" If not, let it go.

Create a calming ritual: A short walk, a warm drink, a few minutes of journaling—something that signals to your brain that it's okay to slow down.

Talk to someone: Anxiety thrives in silence. Sharing your thoughts with a trusted friend, therapist, or even writing them down can reduce their power.

Grounding doesn't erase anxiety, but it gives you a place to stand when the waves come. It reminds you that while your thoughts may race, you don't have to run with them.

Chapter 3
Overthinking Everything

"I'm a perfectionist. I overanalyze everything."

Emma Watson

There's a moment after every decision, every conversation, every text message—when your mind doesn't let go. It replays, rewinds, reanalyzes. You wonder if you said the wrong thing, if you misunderstood, if you missed something. You go over it again and again, hoping to find certainty, but all you find is exhaustion.

Overthinking isn't just thinking too much. It's thinking in circles. It's trying to solve problems that don't exist yet. It's trying to control outcomes that aren't in your hands. And it's one of the most common ways stress, negativity, and loneliness show up in everyday life.

How It Feels

Overthinking feels like:

Mental noise that won't quiet down, even when you're trying to sleep.

Second-guessing everything, from what you wore to what you said.

Feeling stuck, unable to move forward because you're still analyzing the past.

Creating imaginary scenarios, most of them negative, and reacting to them emotionally.

Feeling disconnected, because you're so caught up in your thoughts that you miss the moment.

It's exhausting. It's isolating. And it often feels like you're trying to protect yourself—but instead, you're just wearing yourself out.

Real-Life Examples

Insecurity in Relationships:

Meera sends a message to her partner and doesn't get a reply for hours. Her mind spirals: Did I say something wrong? Are they upset? Are they losing interest? Even though nothing has happened, she feels anxious, restless, and unloved.

Workplace Overthinking:

Ravi gives a presentation at work. It goes well, but afterward, he replays every sentence. Did I sound confident? Did I miss a key point? Did they notice I was nervous? Instead of celebrating, he feels drained and unsure.

Social Overthinking:

Aarav meets friends for dinner. Later, he worries: Did I talk too much? Did I offend someone? Did they enjoy being with me? He texts one of them to "just check," but it's really to soothe his own anxiety.

Loneliness and Overthinking:

Priya spends the weekend alone. She starts thinking: Why don't people reach out? Am I not important? What if I'm always alone? Her thoughts spiral into sadness, even though no one has said or done anything hurtful.

A Principle to Rise: The Principle of Thought Filtering

Overthinking isn't just about having too many thoughts—it's about giving equal weight to all of them. The mind becomes a crowded room where every voice is loud, every worry feels urgent, and every doubt seems true. The way to rise is to filter your thoughts, not fight them. This is the Principle of Thought Filtering.

Thought Filtering means:

Label your thoughts: When a thought arises, ask: Is this a fact, a fear, or a feeling? This helps you separate reality from imagination.

Use the "3-question test":

Is this thought helpful?

Is it kind?

Is it true?

If it fails all three, it doesn't deserve your energy.

Create a "mental parking lot": Write down thoughts that feel urgent but aren't actionable. Revisit them later. This gives your mind permission to let go for now.

Limit your thinking time: Set a timer—10 minutes to reflect, then move on. Overthinking thrives in open-ended mental loops.

Practice "thought distancing": Instead of saying "I'm a failure," say "I'm having the thought that I'm a failure." This small shift creates space between you and your thoughts.

Engage in grounding activities: Do something that requires your full attention—cooking, drawing, walking, solving a puzzle. These help redirect mental energy into the present.

Chapter 4
Panic in Public

"I'm really nervous for something but I forget what... Then I remember it and be nervous. Then I forget again. That is the cycle of my life."

Chrissy Teigen

There's a unique kind of fear that strikes when you're surrounded by people. You're in a market, a classroom, a metro, or a meeting–and suddenly, your heart starts racing. Your chest tightens. Your breath shortens. You feel dizzy, exposed, and desperate to escape. But you can't. You're in public. And panic doesn't care.

Panic in public is terrifying not just because of the physical symptoms, but because of the shame and helplessness that often come with it. You feel like everyone is watching. You worry they'll think you're weak, strange, or unstable. You want to disappear, but you're stuck in the spotlight of your own mind.

How It Feels

Panic in public feels like:

Your body betraying you–sweating, trembling, heart pounding, even when nothing is visibly wrong.

A loss of control–your thoughts race, your breath shortens, and you feel like you might faint or go crazy.

Hyper-awareness—you feel like everyone is staring, judging, noticing your discomfort.

A desperate need to escape, but no safe way to do so.

Shame afterward, wondering why it happened and fearing it will happen again.

It's not just fear—it's fear of fear. And it can make everyday life feel like a minefield.

Real-Life Examples

In a crowded metro:

Ananya is commuting to work when the train suddenly feels too full, too loud, too fast. Her chest tightens. She grips the pole, trying to breathe, but her vision blurs. She wants to get off, but the doors are closed. She feels trapped, terrified, and alone—even though she's surrounded by people.

During a college presentation:

Rohit stands in front of his class. As he begins to speak, his throat dries up. His heart races. He forgets his lines. He feels like he's being watched, judged, laughed at. He rushes through the slides, barely breathing, and leaves the room feeling humiliated.

At a family gathering:

Neha is sitting with relatives when she suddenly feels overwhelmed. The noise, the questions, the attention—it's too much. Her hands shake. She excuses herself to the bathroom, locks the door, and sits on the floor, trying to calm down.

In a supermarket:

Vikram is shopping when he suddenly feels dizzy. His heart pounds. He worries he'll collapse. He abandons his cart and rushes outside, gasping for air. He tells himself it's just stress, but the fear of it happening again keeps him from going back.

A Principle to Rise: The Principle of Safe Exit and Reentry

When panic strikes in public, the instinct is to escape—and that's okay. But healing comes not just from leaving, but from learning how to exit safely and reenter confidently. This is the Principle of Safe Exit and Reentry.

Safe Exit and Reentry means:

Have a calming anchor: Carry something small that grounds you—a smooth stone, a calming scent, a note to yourself. When panic begins, hold it and breathe.

Use a practiced exit strategy: If you need to leave, do so calmly. Say, "I need a moment," or "I'll be right back." This gives you control and dignity.

Find a quiet space: Step outside, into a restroom, or a hallway. Sit, breathe deeply, and remind yourself: "This will pass. I am safe."

Reenter with intention: Once calm, return slowly. Don't rush. Rejoining the moment—even briefly—helps rebuild confidence.

Reflect, don't punish: Afterward, write down what helped and what didn't. Don't shame yourself—celebrate that you managed it.

Build exposure gently: Start with short public outings. Bring a friend. Practice staying a little longer each time. Progress is not perfection—it's persistence.

This principle doesn't promise panic will never return. But it gives you tools to face it, manage it, and slowly reclaim the spaces that fear tried to steal.

Chapter 5
The Fear of Being Judged

"Who are you to judge the life I live? I know I'm not perfect–and I don't live to be–but before you start pointing fingers... make sure your hands are clean!"

Bob Marley

There's a moment before you speak, before you walk into a room, before you post something online–when your heart hesitates. You wonder: What will they think? Will I sound stupid? Will they laugh at me? This is the fear of being judged. It's quiet, but powerful. It shapes how you show up in the world–or whether you show up at all.

This fear doesn't always scream. Sometimes, it whispers: Stay small. Stay quiet. Stay safe. And so, you shrink. You hold back your ideas, your personality, your truth. Not because you don't have something to say–but because you're afraid of how it will be received.

How It Feels

The fear of being judged feels like:

Walking into a room and scanning for approval before you even speak.

Editing yourself constantly, afraid of saying the wrong thing.

Avoiding opportunities, not because you're not capable, but because you're afraid of criticism.

Feeling exposed, even when you're doing something ordinary.

Overthinking interactions, replaying them to check if you were "too much" or "not enough."

It's the fear that people are watching, evaluating, measuring you. And even when they're not, your mind convinces you they are.

Real-Life Examples

In the classroom:

A student knows the answer but doesn't raise their hand. They're afraid of being wrong, of being laughed at, of being "too eager." So they stay silent, even though they had something valuable to share.

At work:

A young employee has an idea that could improve a process, but they don't speak up in the meeting. They worry they'll be dismissed, misunderstood, or seen as trying too hard.

On social media:

Someone wants to share a personal story or creative work, but they hesitate. What if no one likes it? What if people think I'm showing off? So they delete the post before it goes live.

In relationships:

A person avoids expressing their needs or emotions, fearing they'll be seen as needy or dramatic. They bottle things up, trying to be "easy to love," but end up feeling unseen.

A Principle to Rise: The Principle of Inner Approval

When the fear of judgment controls your actions, the solution isn't to silence the world–it's to strengthen your own voice. This is the Principle of Inner Approval.

Inner Approval means:

Know your values: When you act from your values–kindness, honesty, creativity–you build confidence in your choices, regardless of others' reactions.

Practice self-validation: After doing something brave, say to yourself: "I'm proud I showed up." Approval starts within.

Shift the spotlight: Instead of imagining others judging you, imagine them rooting for you. Most people are too focused on themselves to scrutinize you.

Use the "mirror test": Ask: Would I judge someone else for doing what I'm doing? If not, why judge yourself?

Celebrate small acts of courage: Every time you speak up, share something, or show your true self–acknowledge it. Confidence grows through repetition.

Accept imperfection: You will be misunderstood sometimes. You will make mistakes. That's not failure–it's being human.

Inner approval doesn't mean ignoring feedback–it means not depending on it to feel worthy. It's the quiet strength that says: "I know who I am. I trust myself. I belong here."

Chapter 6
Sleepless but Exhausted

"I'm an insomniac, my mind works the night shift."

Pete Wentz

There's a strange contradiction that many people live with: being completely exhausted, yet unable to sleep. You lie in bed, your body aching for rest, but your mind refuses to shut down. Thoughts race. Worries echo. The silence of the night becomes loud with everything you've been trying to ignore during the day.

This isn't just insomnia–it's emotional fatigue. It's the kind of tiredness that sleep alone can't fix. It's the weight of stress, loneliness, and unresolved emotions pressing down on your chest, keeping you awake even when your eyes beg to close.

How It Feels

Sleepless exhaustion feels like:

Lying awake for hours, watching the clock tick, knowing you'll be tired tomorrow.

Feeling drained during the day, but wired at night.

Having a mind that won't stop, even when your body is begging for rest.

Waking up tired, as if sleep never really came.

Feeling emotionally raw, because restlessness amplifies everything—sadness, anxiety, irritability.

It's the kind of fatigue that makes you feel disconnected from yourself. You're too tired to function, but too restless to recover.

Real-Life Examples

The working parent:

Ravi spends his days juggling work and family. By night, he's exhausted—but his mind replays the day, worries about bills, and plans tomorrow's tasks. He lies awake, scrolling his phone, hoping distraction will help. It doesn't.

The student under pressure:

Megha studies late into the night, anxious about exams and expectations. Even when she closes her books, her mind keeps calculating grades, imagining failure, and fearing disappointment. Sleep feels impossible.

The lonely retiree:

Suman lives alone. Her days are quiet, but nights are loud with memories and regrets. She watches TV until late, hoping to feel less alone. But when the screen goes dark, the silence returns—and sleep stays away.

The grieving partner:

Aman lost his spouse months ago. Nights are the hardest. The bed feels too big, the house too quiet. He's tired from crying, from pretending to be okay—but sleep doesn't come. Only memories do.

A Principle to Rise: The Principle of Restful Readiness

When sleep won't come despite exhaustion, the solution isn't just to force rest—it's to prepare the mind and body to receive it. This is the Principle of Restful Readiness.

Restful Readiness means:

Create a wind-down ritual: Choose calming activities before bed—dim lights, soft music, journaling, or reading. Signal to your brain that the day is ending.

Release mental clutter: Write down your worries, tasks, or thoughts. Emptying your mind onto paper helps reduce mental noise.

Avoid stimulation: Limit screens, caffeine, and intense conversations before bed. Replace them with quiet, slow, and soothing inputs.

Use body-based relaxation: Try progressive muscle relaxation—tense and release each muscle group slowly. This helps shift your body into rest mode.

Practice acceptance: Instead of fighting sleeplessness, accept it gently. Say, "It's okay if I don't sleep right away. I'm still resting." This reduces pressure and anxiety.

Anchor yourself in comfort: Surround yourself with things that feel safe—soft blankets, calming scents, a favorite book. Comfort invites rest.

Restful readiness isn't about perfect sleep—it's about creating space for rest to return. It's about honoring your exhaustion with kindness, not frustration. And it's about trusting that healing often begins in stillness, even before sleep arrives.

Chapter 7
The Shame Spiral

"We're not taught how to process shame and guilt.
I've never in my life ever used the Pythagorean theorem!"

Iyanla Vanzant

Shame doesn't knock–it slips in quietly. It starts with a mistake, a moment of vulnerability, or a memory you wish you could erase. Then it grows. It tells you that you're not just someone who did something wrong–you are something wrong. And before you know it, you're spiraling.

The shame spiral is a mental and emotional loop where one painful thought leads to another, and another, until you're buried under the weight of self-blame. It's not just about guilt–it's about identity. It convinces you that your flaws define you, that your past disqualifies you, and that you're unworthy of love, success, or peace.

How It Feels

The shame spiral feels like:

Replaying a moment over and over, each time feeling worse about it.

Avoiding people, not because they've judged you–but because you've already judged yourself.

Feeling exposed, even when no one knows what happened.

Believing you're broken, not just flawed.

Wanting to disappear, not out of drama, but out of deep emotional fatigue.

It's the voice in your head that says, "You're not good enough. You always mess things up. You'll never change." And the more you listen, the more you believe it.

Real-Life Examples

The job interview that went wrong:

After stumbling through an interview, Arjun can't stop thinking about how he froze when asked a question. He replays it for days, convinced he looked foolish. He starts doubting his skills, avoids applying for other jobs, and tells himself he's not cut out for success.

The argument with a friend:

Ritika snapped at her best friend during a stressful week. Even after apologizing, she can't forgive herself. She avoids texts, convinced her friend secretly resents her. The shame grows louder than the actual conflict ever was.

The social media post:

Karan shared something personal online and received a few sarcastic comments. He deleted the post, but the shame lingers. He tells himself he overshared, that people are laughing at him, and that he should never open up again.

The childhood memory:

Even years later, Meena still remembers being laughed at in school for mispronouncing a word. It was a small moment, but it planted a seed of shame that still makes her afraid to speak up in groups.

A Principle to Rise: The Principle of Self-Reclamation

Shame thrives in silence and secrecy. It grows when we hide. The way to rise is not to erase the past, but to reclaim your story—with compassion, not condemnation. This is the Principle of Self-Reclamation.

Self-Reclamation means:

Name the shame: Say it out loud or write it down. "I feel ashamed because..." Naming it breaks its power.

Separate action from identity: You made a mistake. You are not a mistake. One moment doesn't define your worth.

Speak to yourself like a friend: Would you say to someone else what you're saying to yourself? If not, rewrite the script.

Find a safe witness: Share your story with someone who listens without judgment. Shame shrinks when it's seen with empathy.

Reframe the narrative: Instead of "I failed," say "I learned." Instead of "I'm broken," say "I'm healing."

Re-enter the world: Shame wants you to hide. Healing begins when you show up anyway—imperfect, but present.

Self-reclamation isn't about pretending the pain didn't happen. It's about choosing to believe that you are more than your worst moment. That you are still worthy. Still growing. Still here.

Chapter 8
Feeling Like a Burden

"You only have the burdens on you that you choose to put there."

Brandon Lee

There's a quiet pain that doesn't always show on the surface. It's not loud like anger or sharp like panic. It's heavier. It's the feeling that your presence is too much, your needs are inconvenient, and your struggles are a weight others shouldn't have to carry. It's the belief that you are a burden.

This feeling doesn't always come from what people say–it often comes from what they don't. A delayed reply, a tired sigh, a distracted look. Your mind fills in the blanks: They're tired of me. I'm asking for too much. I should just deal with this alone.

How It Feels

Feeling like a burden feels like:

Apologizing for expressing your emotions, even when you're hurting.

Withholding your needs, because you don't want to "bother" anyone.

Overthinking every message, wondering if you're being too much.

Avoiding asking for help, even when you desperately need it.

Feeling invisible, not because no one sees you—but because you've convinced yourself you shouldn't be seen.

It's the kind of heaviness that makes you isolate yourself—not because you want to be alone, but because you believe others are better off without your pain.

Real-Life Examples

The friend who cancels plans:

Aarav has been feeling low for weeks. He wants to talk to someone, but every time he picks up the phone, he puts it down. They're busy. They have their own problems. I don't want to drag them down. So he cancels plans and says he's "just tired."

The caregiver who never asks for help:

Sunita takes care of her aging parents and her children. She's overwhelmed, but when friends offer support, she smiles and says, "I'm fine." Inside, she's drowning—but she believes asking for help would make her a burden.

The partner who hides their struggles:

Rohan is going through a tough time at work. He doesn't tell his partner because he doesn't want to "add stress." He becomes distant, not out of anger, but out of fear that his pain will push them away.

The student who stays silent:

Mehak is struggling with anxiety but doesn't tell her teacher or parents. She thinks, "They'll just worry. I should be able to handle this." So she suffers in silence, her grades slipping, her energy fading.

A Principle to Rise: The Principle of Shared Humanity

When you feel like a burden, the instinct is to retreat. But healing begins when you remember that you are not a problem to be solved—

you are a person to be supported. This is the Principle of Shared Humanity.

Shared Humanity means:

Recognize the lie: The belief that you're a burden is not truth–it's shame in disguise. Challenge it gently.

Remember how you care for others: Think of someone you love. Would you want them to hide their pain from you? Then why should you?

Let others choose: Don't decide for people that they can't handle your truth. Give them the chance to show up for you.

Start small: Share one honest sentence. "I'm not okay today." Let that be enough.

Accept help without guilt: Receiving support doesn't make you weak–it makes you human. And it gives others the gift of being there for you.

Reframe connection: You're not a burden–you're a bridge. Your vulnerability invites closeness, not distance.

Shared humanity reminds us that we all carry something. And sometimes, the most healing thing we can do is let someone carry a little of it with us.

Chapter 9
The Pressure to Be "Fine"

"I found that with depression, one of the most important things you could realize is that you're not alone."

Dwayne "The Rock" Johnson

There's a phrase we say almost automatically: "I'm fine." It slips out in conversations, texts, meetings, and family dinners. Sometimes we say it because we don't want to explain. Sometimes we say it because we don't think anyone really wants to know. And sometimes, we say it because we've convinced ourselves that we should be fine—even when we're not.

The pressure to be "fine" is a quiet kind of suffering. It's the emotional mask we wear to keep others comfortable, to avoid being seen as weak, or to protect ourselves from vulnerability. It's the belief that expressing pain is a burden, that struggling is failure, and that silence is strength.

How It Feels

The pressure to be "fine" feels like:

Smiling when you want to cry, because you don't want to make things awkward.

Saying "I'm okay", even when your chest feels heavy and your thoughts are loud.

Feeling disconnected, because no one knows what you're really going through.

Avoiding honesty, because you fear being judged, pitied, or misunderstood.

Carrying emotional weight alone, because asking for help feels like admitting defeat.

It's the kind of pressure that makes you perform wellness instead of pursuing it. You become an actor in your own life, rehearsing lines of strength while hiding scenes of struggle.

Real-Life Examples

At work:

Riya is overwhelmed with deadlines and personal stress, but when her manager asks how she's doing, she says, "All good!" She doesn't want to seem incapable. She pushes through, but her performance suffers, and her burnout deepens.

In friendships:

Aman hasn't been feeling like himself for weeks. His friends invite him out, and he goes, laughing and chatting. But afterward, he feels emptier than before. He wants to talk about what's really going on, but he fears they'll pull away.

In family settings:

Mehak is struggling with anxiety, but when her parents ask how she's doing, she says, "I'm fine." She doesn't want to worry them. She keeps her pain hidden, even though she longs for comfort.

On social media:

Karan posts smiling selfies and motivational quotes, but behind the screen, he's battling loneliness. He feels like he has to maintain a positive image, even when his reality is far from it.

A Principle to Rise: The Principle of Honest Presence

When the pressure to be "fine" becomes a daily performance, the way to rise is not to abandon strength–but to redefine it. This is the Principle of Honest Presence.

Honest Presence means:

Replace "I'm fine" with truth in layers: You don't have to share everything. But try saying, "I've had better days," or "I'm managing, but it's been tough." Honesty builds connection.

Choose safe spaces: Not everyone deserves your vulnerability. But someone does. Find those people and let them in.

Practice emotional check-ins: Ask yourself daily, "How am I really?" Write it down. Speak it aloud. Let your truth breathe.

Let go of perfection: You don't have to be okay all the time. You don't have to be strong in every moment. You just have to be real.

Model openness: When you share your truth, you give others permission to do the same. Vulnerability is contagious–in the best way.

Redefine strength: Strength isn't silence. It's showing up with your truth, even when it's messy. It's choosing honesty over image.

Honest presence doesn't mean being raw with everyone–it means being real with yourself, and with those who matter. It's the quiet courage to say, "I'm not fine. And that's okay."

Chapter 10
When You Can't Breathe but You're Still Smiling

"I think the saddest people always try their hardest to make people happy. Because they know what it feels like to feel absolutely worthless."

Robin Williams

There's a kind of pain that hides behind a smile. You show up, you laugh, you say you're okay–but inside, it feels like you're gasping for air. You're overwhelmed, anxious, and emotionally drained, but you keep performing wellness because it's what's expected. You smile, not because you're fine, but because you don't know how to say you're not.

This is the paradox of emotional suffocation: appearing composed while feeling like you're falling apart. It's the pressure to maintain a mask of strength while your inner world is unraveling. And it's more common than we think.

How It Feels

Smiling while struggling feels like:

Pretending to be okay, even when your chest feels tight and your thoughts are racing.

Feeling disconnected from your own emotions, because you've suppressed them for so long.

Being praised for your strength, while secretly wishing someone would notice your pain.

Feeling guilty for not being "grateful enough", even when you're hurting.

Wanting someone to ask how you really are, but fearing what might happen if you tell the truth.

It's the kind of emotional exhaustion that makes you feel invisible in plain sight. You're surrounded by people, but no one sees the storm inside.

Real-Life Examples

At work:

Neha is the "go-to" person in her office—always smiling, always helpful. But behind the scenes, she's battling anxiety and burnout. She cries in the bathroom, wipes her tears, and returns with a smile. No one knows. She doesn't let them.

In friendships:

Aarav is the funny one in his group. He cracks jokes, lifts others up, and never complains. But at night, he lies awake, feeling empty. He doesn't want to "bring the mood down," so he keeps smiling—even when it hurts.

In family life:

Parleen is the emotional anchor of her family. She listens to everyone's problems, offers advice, and keeps things together. But she hasn't told anyone that she feels like she's drowning. She's afraid they'll worry. So she keeps smiling.

On social media:

Karan posts happy photos and motivational quotes. People comment, "You're so inspiring!" But they don't see the panic attacks, the sleepless nights, the quiet breakdowns. He feels like he's living two lives—one online, one alone.

A Principle to Rise: The Principle of Emotional Permission

When you feel like you can't breathe but still have to smile, the way to rise is not to abandon your strength—but to give yourself permission to feel. This is the Principle of Emotional Permission.

Emotional Permission means:

Allow yourself to feel without judgment: Sadness, fear, anger—none of these make you weak. They make you human.

Create a space for truth: Find one person, one journal, one moment where you can be completely honest. Let your mask down.

Stop apologizing for your emotions: You don't owe anyone constant positivity. You owe yourself authenticity.

Practice emotional honesty in small doses: Say, "I'm having a tough day," or "I'm not feeling like myself." Let that be enough.

Recognize the cost of constant performance: Smiling through pain may protect others—but it isolates you. Choose connection over perfection.

Let your healing be visible: You don't have to be "fixed" to be seen. You just have to be real.

Emotional permission is the quiet courage to say, "I'm not okay right now, and I don't have to pretend." It's the first step toward breathing freely again—not behind a smile, but through your truth.

Part two

The Mind's Maze

Chapter 1
Negative Thought Loops

"If you realized how powerful your thoughts are,
you would never think a negative thought."

Peace Pilgrim

There's a moment when a single negative thought enters your mind–and instead of passing through, it settles in. It repeats. It grows. It pulls in other thoughts, other memories, other fears. Before you know it, you're stuck in a loop. You're not just thinking–you're spiraling.

Negative thought loops are patterns of repetitive, self-defeating thinking. They often start with a trigger–an awkward moment, a mistake, a fear–and then cycle through doubt, shame, and anxiety. These loops don't just affect your mood; they shape your perception of yourself, your relationships, and your future.

How It Feels

Being trapped in a negative thought loop feels like:

Replaying the same scenario over and over, hoping to find a different outcome.

Feeling stuck in your head, unable to focus on the present.

Questioning your worth, even over small mistakes.

Imagining worst-case scenarios, even when nothing is wrong.

Feeling emotionally drained, as if your mind is working against you.

It's like being caught in a mental echo chamber—where every thought reinforces the last, and escape feels impossible.

Real-Life Examples

After a social interaction:

Mehak leaves a party and immediately starts replaying everything she said. Did I talk too much? Did I offend someone? Did they think I was awkward? She spends the night analyzing every word, unable to sleep.

At work:

Ravi makes a small error in a report. His manager corrects it kindly, but Ravi's mind spirals: I'm not good enough. I always mess up. What if I lose my job? The mistake becomes a story about his entire identity.

In relationships:

Aarav texts his partner and doesn't get a reply for hours. His mind loops: They're upset. I said something wrong. Maybe they're pulling away. Even though nothing has happened, the loop creates emotional chaos.

During quiet moments:

Karan sits alone on a Sunday afternoon. Instead of relaxing, his mind drifts to past failures, missed opportunities, and fears about the future. The silence becomes a breeding ground for self-doubt.

A Principle to Rise: The Principle of Thought Disruption

When negative thought loops take over, the goal isn't to suppress them—it's to interrupt them. This is the Principle of Thought Disruption.

Thought Disruption means:

Catch the loop early: Notice when a thought starts repeating. Say to yourself, "I've thought this already. It's time to pause."

Change the channel: Shift your focus with a physical action–stand up, stretch, drink water, step outside. Movement breaks mental momentum.

Use a pattern breaker: Ask a disruptive question like, "What's the evidence for this thought?" or "What would I say to a friend feeling this way?"

Limit rumination time: Set a timer–5 minutes to reflect, then move on. Give your thoughts boundaries.

Replace with a grounding truth: Choose one statement that calms you. "I made a mistake, but I'm learning." "I don't know the future, but I'm safe right now."

Practice mental redirection: Engage in something that requires focus–reading, cooking, solving a puzzle. Redirecting attention helps reset the loop.

Thought disruption isn't about denying your emotions–it's about reclaiming control over your mental space. It's the gentle art of saying, "I hear you, mind–but I'm choosing a different path."

Chapter 2
The Inner Critic

"People often miss out on their own human genius because they're trying to be more perfect than the gods."

Curtis Tyrone Jones

There's a voice inside your head that doesn't shout–it whispers. It questions your worth, criticizes your choices, and reminds you of every flaw. It's not the voice of reason or reflection–it's the inner critic. And for many, it's louder than any external judgment.

The inner critic doesn't just appear when you make a mistake. It shows up when you try something new, when you speak your truth, when you dare to hope. It's the voice that says, "You're not good enough." "You'll fail." "Why even try?" And the worst part? It often sounds like you.

How It Feels

Living with a harsh inner critic feels like:

Constant self-doubt, even when you're doing well.

Feeling like an imposter, no matter how much you've achieved.

Over-apologizing, because you assume you're always wrong.

Avoiding risks, because failure feels inevitable.

Never feeling “enough”, no matter how hard you try.

It’s like carrying a mirror that only reflects your flaws. You start to believe that your mistakes define you, that your weaknesses outweigh your strengths, and that your voice doesn’t deserve to be heard.

Real-Life Examples

In creative work:

Mehak wants to start a blog. She writes a few posts but never publishes them. Her inner critic says, “No one will read this. You’re not a real writer.” So she keeps her words hidden, even though they could help someone else.

At work:

Ravi gets positive feedback from his manager, but his inner critic says, “They’re just being nice. You don’t really deserve it.” He downplays his success and avoids applying for a promotion.

In relationships:

Aarav feels anxious about expressing his needs to his partner. His inner critic says, “You’re too needy. You’ll push them away.” So he stays silent, even when he’s hurting.

In parenting:

Sunita is doing her best to raise her children, but every time she loses patience, her inner critic says, “You’re a bad mother.” She feels guilty, even though she’s loving and present.

A Principle to Rise: The Principle of Inner Reparenting

To quiet the inner critic, you don’t need to fight it–you need to reparent it. This is the Principle of Inner Reparenting.

Inner Reparenting means:

Recognize the voice: Notice when the inner critic speaks. Ask, "Whose voice is this?" Often, it echoes past experiences—not present truths.

Respond with compassion: Instead of arguing, offer kindness. Say, "I'm learning. I'm allowed to grow. I'm doing my best."

Create a new inner voice: Imagine how a loving parent or mentor would speak to you. Practice using that voice in moments of doubt.

Challenge the narrative: Ask, "Is this thought helpful? Is it true? What's the evidence?" Replace criticism with curiosity.

Celebrate small wins: Every time you show up, try again, or speak kindly to yourself—acknowledge it. Confidence grows through repetition.

Build emotional safety: Surround yourself with people who affirm your worth. Let their kindness help reshape your inner dialogue.

Inner reparenting isn't about ignoring your flaws—it's about nurturing your growth. It's choosing to speak to yourself with the same love, patience, and encouragement you'd offer to someone you care about deeply.

Chapter 3
Comparing Yourself to Everyone

"The reason we struggle with insecurity is because we compare our behind-the-scenes with everyone else's highlight reel."

Steven Furtick

It starts subtly. You scroll through social media and see someone's vacation, someone's promotion, someone's perfect relationship. You glance at your own life and feel a pang. You tell yourself it's harmless, just curiosity. But soon, it becomes a habit. You measure your worth against others' highlights. You start believing you're behind, less successful, less lovable. You start comparing yourself to everyone.

Comparison is one of the most common traps in the mind's maze. It doesn't just steal joy—it distorts reality. It convinces you that your journey is invalid because it doesn't look like someone else's. It makes you forget that what you see is rarely the full story.

How It Feels

Constant comparison feels like:

Feeling inadequate, even when you're doing well.

Doubting your progress, because someone else seems ahead.

Resenting your own life, not because it's bad—but because it's not "as good."

Feeling stuck, because you're chasing someone else's timeline.

Losing sight of your own values, because you're trying to match someone else's goals.

It's the kind of mental fog that makes you question your worth, your choices, and your pace. You stop celebrating your wins because they don't look like someone else's.

Real-Life Examples

On social media:

Mehak sees her college friend posting about a new job abroad. She's happy for her, but also feels like she's falling behind. She starts questioning her own career path, even though she was content with it just yesterday.

In relationships:

Ravi sees couples posting anniversary photos and romantic gestures. He starts feeling insecure about his own relationship, wondering if it's lacking—even though it's built on quiet, steady love.

In parenting:

Sunita compares herself to other moms who seem to have it all together—craft projects, clean homes, smiling kids. She feels guilty for struggling, even though she's doing her best every single day.

In creative work:

Aarav is an artist who sees others selling their work online, gaining followers, getting recognition. He starts doubting his talent, even though creating art brings him peace.

A Principle to Rise: The Principle of Personal Alignment

To escape the comparison trap, you don't need to ignore others—you need to realign with yourself. This is the Principle of Personal Alignment.

Personal Alignment means:

Define your own success: Ask yourself, "What does a meaningful life look like for me?" Let your values guide your goals.

Limit passive consumption: Reduce time spent scrolling through curated lives. Choose content that inspires, not pressures.

Celebrate your timeline: Remind yourself, "I'm not late. I'm on my path." Progress isn't a race—it's a rhythm.

Practice gratitude for your journey: Write down three things you're proud of each week. Focus on growth, not comparison.

Use comparison as reflection, not judgment: If someone's life triggers envy, ask, "What does this reveal about what I want?" Then take one step toward it.

Reconnect with your strengths: Make a list of what makes you unique—skills, experiences, values. Let that be your compass.

Personal alignment isn't about ignoring others—it's about remembering that your life is not a competition. It's a creation. And you are the artist.

Chapter 4
Imposter Syndrome

"You think, 'Why would anyone want to see me again in a movie? And I don't know how to act anyway, so why am I doing this?"

Meryl Streep

"Sometimes I wake up in the morning before going off to a shoot, and I think, I can't do this."

Kate Winslet

You've worked hard. You've achieved something meaningful. People praise you, admire your work, and trust your abilities. But inside, you feel like a fraud. You think, "I just got lucky." "They don't know the truth." "One day, they'll find out I'm not good enough." This is Imposter Syndrome–the persistent belief that you're not truly capable, despite evidence to the contrary.

Imposter Syndrome doesn't just affect high achievers–it affects anyone who feels like they don't belong in the space they've earned. It's the mental trap that convinces you your success is undeserved, your confidence is fake, and your presence is temporary.

How It Feels

Imposter Syndrome feels like:

Dismissing compliments, because you don't believe you deserve them.

Over-preparing, because you fear being exposed as incompetent.

Feeling like you're faking it, even when you're doing well.

Avoiding new opportunities, because you think you're not ready.

Living with constant anxiety, waiting for the moment you'll be "found out."

It's the kind of self-doubt that doesn't go away with achievement—it grows with it. The more you succeed, the more pressure you feel to maintain the illusion.

Real-Life Examples

In academics:

Mehak gets accepted into a prestigious university. Her classmates seem confident, articulate, and well-prepared. She feels out of place, convinced she got in by mistake. She studies obsessively, afraid of being exposed.

At work:

Ravi is promoted to a leadership role. His team respects him, but he feels like he's pretending. Every decision feels like a test. He avoids giving feedback, fearing he's not qualified to lead.

In creative fields:

Aarav publishes his first book. Readers love it, but he feels like he tricked them. He avoids interviews, fearing he won't sound "smart enough." He starts doubting whether he should write another.

In parenting:

Sunita is raising two children. She's doing her best, but every time she makes a mistake, she thinks, "I'm not cut out for this." She compares herself to other parents and feels like she's failing—even though her children are thriving.

A Principle to Rise: The Principle of Identity Integration

To overcome Imposter Syndrome, you don't need to prove yourself more—you need to integrate your identity with your reality. This is the Principle of Identity Integration.

Identity Integration means:

Acknowledge your achievements: Keep a record of things you've done well—projects completed, compliments received, goals reached. Let facts challenge your feelings.

Separate feelings from facts: Feeling like a fraud doesn't mean you are one. Emotions are valid, but they're not always accurate.

Speak your truth aloud: Say, "I worked hard for this." "I belong here." "I'm learning, and that's enough." Repetition builds belief.

Normalize growth: You don't have to know everything. Being in progress doesn't mean you're an imposter—it means you're human.

Connect with others who feel the same: Talk to peers, mentors, or friends. You'll discover that many successful people feel the same way—and that you're not alone.

Redefine competence: Competence isn't perfection—it's showing up, learning, and improving. You don't have to be flawless to be worthy.

Identity integration is about aligning who you are with what you've earned. It's about letting go of the fear that you're pretending—and embracing the truth that you're becoming.

Chapter 5
The Fear of Failure

"I've failed over and over and over again in my life.
And that is why I succeed."

Michael Jordan

There's a moment before you begin—before you apply, speak up, take a risk—when your heart hesitates. You imagine everything that could go wrong. You picture embarrassment, rejection, disappointment. And so, you freeze. You tell yourself, "Maybe later." "I'm not ready." "What if I fail?" This is the fear of failure—quiet, persistent, and deeply limiting.

The fear of failure doesn't just stop you from trying—it convinces you that trying isn't worth it. It makes you believe that mistakes define you, that setbacks are shameful, and that imperfection is unacceptable. It's not just fear of the outcome—it's fear of what the outcome says about you.

How It Feels

The fear of failure feels like:

Avoiding opportunities, even ones you secretly want.

Overthinking every step, trying to guarantee success before you begin.

Procrastinating, not because you're lazy, but because you're afraid.

Feeling paralyzed, stuck between desire and dread.

Judging yourself harshly, even before anything goes wrong.

It's the kind of fear that makes you shrink your dreams, silence your voice, and settle for less—not because you don't care, but because you care too much.

Real-Life Examples

In academics:

Mehak wants to apply for a scholarship but doesn't. She fears rejection. She tells herself she's not qualified, even though she meets every requirement. The fear of failing keeps her from even trying.

At work:

Ravi has an idea that could improve his team's workflow. But he doesn't share it. He worries it won't be received well, that he'll be criticized. So he stays quiet, and the idea stays hidden.

In creative pursuits:

Aarav dreams of starting a podcast. He records a few episodes but never publishes them. He fears people won't listen, won't care, or will judge him. The fear of failure becomes stronger than the desire to create.

In relationships:

Sunita wants to express her feelings to someone she cares about. But she holds back. She fears rejection, awkwardness, or ruining the connection. So she stays silent, and the moment passes.

A Principle to Rise: The Principle of Courageous Permission

To overcome the fear of failure, you don't need to eliminate fear—you need to give yourself permission to fail. This is the Principle of Courageous Permission.

Courageous Permission means:

Redefine failure: Failure isn't the opposite of success–it's part of it. Every setback is a step forward in disguise.

Shift the goal: Instead of aiming for perfection, aim for progress. Ask, "What can I learn?" not "What if I lose?"

Take micro-risks: Start small. Share one idea. Apply for one opportunity. Speak one truth. Build your courage in layers.

Celebrate effort, not outcome: Applaud yourself for showing up, regardless of the result. Effort is always a win.

Use failure as feedback: When something doesn't work, ask, "What is this teaching me?" Let failure refine you, not define you.

Surround yourself with support: Share your fears with people who uplift you. Courage grows in connection.

Courageous permission is the quiet strength to say, "I might fail–and I'll be okay." It's the decision to live boldly, not perfectly. Because the only true failure is never trying at all.

Chapter 6
The Fear of Success

"My therapist says I'm afraid of success. I guess I could understand that, because after all, fulfilling my potential would really cut into my sitting-around time."

Maria Bamford

It sounds contradictory—why would anyone fear success? Isn't that what we're all striving for? But for many, success doesn't feel like a reward. It feels like a risk. A threat. A pressure. The fear of success is subtle, often mistaken for procrastination, self-sabotage, or "not being ready." But underneath, it's the anxiety that success will bring expectations, visibility, responsibility—and maybe even isolation.

This fear isn't about doubting your ability to succeed. The fear of success is the anxiety or discomfort that arises not from failing—but from *actually achieving* your goals. It sounds counterintuitive, but many people subconsciously sabotage their own progress because success can feel overwhelming, isolating, or even threatening.

How It Feels

The fear of success feels like:

Holding back, even when you know you're capable.

Sabotaging opportunities, because you're afraid of what comes next.

Feeling anxious about recognition, because it brings attention and pressure.

Avoiding growth, because it might mean leaving comfort zones or relationships behind.

Feeling guilty for wanting more, as if ambition is selfish or dangerous.

It's the kind of fear that makes you shrink your dreams—not because you don't believe in them, but because you're afraid of what they'll demand from you.

Real-Life Examples

In career growth:

Mehak is offered a promotion. She's qualified, excited, and proud. But she hesitates. Will I be able to handle it? Will my coworkers treat me differently? Will I lose my work-life balance? She declines, telling herself it's not the right time.

In creative pursuits:

Ravi's artwork gains attention online. People want to buy his pieces, invite him to exhibitions. But he stops posting. He fears the pressure to keep producing, the judgment that might come with visibility. He tells himself he's "just doing it for fun."

In academics:

Aarav is top of his class. Teachers encourage him to apply to prestigious universities. But he delays. He fears leaving home, being seen as "too ambitious," and not living up to expectations. He chooses a safer path, even though he dreams bigger.

In personal growth:

Sunita starts therapy and begins healing. She feels better, stronger. But she worries: Will my family understand? Will they think I've changed too much? She slows down her progress, afraid of outgrowing the people she loves.

A Principle to Rise: The Principle of Worthy Expansion

To overcome the fear of success, you don't need to chase achievement–you need to embrace your right to grow. This is the Principle of Worthy Expansion.

Worthy Expansion means:

Redefine success as alignment: Success isn't about status–it's about living in alignment with your values, passions, and truth.

Normalize growth: You're allowed to evolve. Growth doesn't mean abandoning others–it means becoming more of who you are.

Prepare for visibility with boundaries: Success may bring attention, but you can choose what to share, how to show up, and when to rest.

Challenge guilt with gratitude: When guilt arises, replace it with gratitude. "I'm grateful for this opportunity. I will honor it with care."

Visualize sustainable success: Imagine success that feels safe, balanced, and authentic. Let go of the myth that success must be overwhelming.

Affirm your worth daily: Say, "I am worthy of growth. I am allowed to succeed. I can rise without losing myself."

Worthy expansion is the quiet permission to grow without fear. It's the belief that success doesn't have to cost your peace, your relationships, or your identity. It can be gentle, intentional, and deeply fulfilling.

Chapter 7
Perfectionism's Trap

"Perfectionism is the voice of the oppressor, the enemy of the people. It will keep you cramped and insane your whole life."

Anne Lamott

Perfectionism often wears a disguise. It looks like ambition, discipline, high standards. It's praised, rewarded, even admired. But beneath the surface, it's a trap. It's not about doing things well–it's about never feeling like you've done enough. It's the belief that anything less than perfect is failure. And it's exhausting.

Perfectionism doesn't just affect your work–it affects your self-worth. It convinces you that your value is tied to flawless performance, constant productivity, and the absence of mistakes. It makes rest feel guilty, vulnerability feel weak, and progress feel inadequate.

How It Feels

Perfectionism feels like:

Never being satisfied, even when others praise your work.

Overworking, because you fear falling short.

Avoiding tasks, because you're afraid you won't do them perfectly.

Feeling anxious about small mistakes, as if they define your entire worth.

Struggling to celebrate wins, because you only see what could've been better.

It's the kind of mindset that turns every effort into a test, every achievement into a checklist, and every flaw into a personal failure.

Real-Life Examples

In academics:

Mehak gets top grades but feels crushed by a single B. She studies obsessively, not out of passion, but out of fear. She believes anything less than perfect means she's not smart enough.

At work:

Ravi spends hours refining a presentation that was already good. He misses sleep, skips meals, and still feels it's not "ready." He fears being judged, even though his team trusts him.

In creative pursuits:

Aarav writes poetry but never shares it. He edits endlessly, convinced it's not good enough. He compares himself to published authors and tells himself he's not "real" until it's flawless.

In parenting:

Sunita tries to be the perfect mother–healthy meals, clean house, emotionally present. When she loses patience one day, she spirals into guilt. She feels like she's failing, even though her children feel loved.

A Principle to Rise: The Principle of Compassionate Completion

To escape perfectionism's trap, you don't need to lower your standards—you need to complete with compassion. This is the Principle of Compassionate Completion.

Compassionate Completion means:

Redefine "done": Done doesn't mean flawless—it means finished with care and intention. Let go of endless tweaking.

Honor effort over outcome: Ask, "Did I show up fully?" not "Was it perfect?" Effort is a reflection of growth.

Set realistic boundaries: Give yourself time limits. When the timer ends, the task ends. Completion builds momentum.

Practice self-kindness: When you make a mistake, say, "I'm learning. I'm human. I'm allowed to grow."

Celebrate imperfect wins: Share your work, your voice, your progress—even if it's not perfect. Visibility builds courage.

Rest without guilt: Rest is not a reward for perfection—it's a requirement for sustainability. You deserve it.

Compassionate completion is the quiet strength to say, "This is enough. I am enough." It's the shift from chasing perfection to embracing progress—with grace, patience, and self-respect.

Chapter 8
Self-Doubt That Sticks

"The greater the artist, the greater the doubt. Perfect confidence is granted to the less talented as a consolation prize."

Robert Hughes

Self-doubt doesn't always arrive loudly. Sometimes, it creeps in quietly and stays. It doesn't just question your choices–it questions your worth. It's the voice that says, "Are you sure you can do this?" "What if you're not good enough?" "What if they find out you're not who they think you are?" And even when you succeed, it whispers, "You just got lucky."

This kind of self-doubt isn't fleeting–it's sticky. It clings to your thoughts, your decisions, your identity. It makes you second-guess your instincts, delay your dreams, and shrink your voice. And the longer it stays, the more it feels like truth.

How It Feels

Sticky self-doubt feels like:

Questioning your abilities, even when you've proven them.

Feeling like a fraud, despite external validation.

Overthinking every decision, fearing you'll mess up.

Avoiding risks, because failure feels inevitable.

Seeking constant reassurance, but never feeling reassured.

It's the kind of mental fog that makes you feel stuck in place–wanting to move forward, but unsure if you're allowed to.

Real-Life Examples

In academics:

Mehak gets good grades but still feels like she's not smart enough. Every time she's called on in class, her heart races. She prepares obsessively, not out of confidence, but out of fear of being exposed.

At work:

Ravi is praised for his performance, but he still doubts himself. He avoids taking on new projects, convinced he'll eventually fail. He watches others grow and wonders why he can't believe in himself.

In relationships:

Aarav is in a loving relationship, but he constantly wonders if he's "too much" or "not enough." He fears being left, not because of anything his partner has done, but because he doubts his own worth.

In creative pursuits:

Sunita writes poetry but never shares it. She reads others' work and thinks, "Mine isn't good enough." She dreams of publishing but convinces herself she's not ready–maybe she never will be.

A Principle to Rise: The Principle of Self-Trust Restoration

To overcome sticky self-doubt, you don't need to silence it–you need to rebuild trust in yourself. This is the Principle of Self-Trust Restoration.

Self-Trust Restoration means:

Track your truth: Keep a journal of moments when you showed up, succeeded, or made a brave choice. Let your history challenge your doubt.

Speak to yourself with authority: Say, "I've done hard things before. I can do this too." Confidence grows through repetition.

Take small, bold steps: Don't wait to feel ready. Act in spite of doubt. Each step builds evidence that you can trust yourself.

Limit comparison: Your path is yours. Comparing it to others only fuels doubt. Focus on your growth, not their timeline.

Practice self-validation: Before seeking reassurance, ask yourself, "What do I know to be true about me?" Let your own voice lead.

Accept imperfection: You don't need to be flawless to be worthy. Mistakes don't erase your value–they prove you're learning.

Self-trust restoration is the quiet decision to believe in yourself again–not because you're perfect, but because you're present, persistent, and growing. It's the shift from "I'm not sure I can" to "I'll find out by trying."

Chapter 9
The Voice That Says "You're Not Enough"

"You've been criticizing yourself for years and it hasn't worked. Try approving of yourself and see what happens."

Louise Hay

"Talk to yourself like you would to someone you love."

Brené Brown

There's a voice inside that doesn't yell–it whispers. It shows up when you're trying something new, when you're standing in front of others, when you're alone with your thoughts. It says, "You're not enough." Not smart enough. Not attractive enough. Not successful enough. Not lovable enough. And the worst part? You start to believe it.

This voice isn't always loud, but it's persistent. It doesn't just question your abilities–it questions your worth. It turns every compliment into doubt, every achievement into luck, and every setback into proof. It's the voice that keeps you small, quiet, and uncertain–even when the world is ready to hear you.

How It Feels

The "not enough" voice feels like:

Constant comparison, where you always come up short.

Dismissing praise, because you don't believe you deserve it.

Feeling invisible, even when you're surrounded by people.

Overcompensating, trying to prove your worth through perfection or productivity.

Avoiding vulnerability, because you fear being truly seen.

It's the kind of inner dialogue that makes you question your place in the world. You start to wonder if you're worthy of love, success, or even rest.

Real-Life Examples

In relationships:

Mehak is in a loving relationship, but she constantly worries she's not enough for her partner. She overthinks every interaction, fears being left, and feels she has to earn love through constant effort.

At work:

Ravi gets positive feedback but still feels inadequate. He works overtime, avoids asking for help, and fears being exposed as "not capable." Even when he's praised, he feels like he's falling short.

In social settings:

Aarav avoids speaking up in groups. He fears his thoughts aren't valuable, that others are smarter or more interesting. He stays quiet, even when he has something meaningful to say.

In personal growth:

Sunita starts therapy and begins healing, but she still hears the voice that says, "You're too broken." She doubts her progress, feels guilty for needing help, and wonders if she'll ever be "whole."

A Principle to Rise: The Principle of Enoughness

To quiet the voice that says "you're not enough," you don't need to become more–you need to recognize that you already are. This is the Principle of Enoughness.

Enoughness means:

Challenge the voice: When it speaks, ask, "Who taught me this?" and "Is it true?" Most of the time, it's not.

Affirm your worth daily: Say, "I am enough as I am." Not because you've achieved something–but because you exist.

Celebrate your being, not just your doing: You are valuable even when you're resting, struggling, or simply being.

Practice self-acceptance: Make space for your flaws, your quirks, your humanity. You don't need to be perfect to be worthy.

Surround yourself with truth-tellers: Spend time with people who see your light, not just your effort. Let their love reflect your worth.

Redefine success: Success isn't being more–it's being real. It's living in alignment with your values, not someone else's expectations.

Enoughness is the quiet revolution of choosing self-worth over self-doubt. It's the decision to stop chasing approval and start embracing authenticity. It's the truth that you don't have to earn your place–you already belong.

Chapter 10
Wanting to Disappear

"I think everybody should get rich and famous and do everything they ever dreamed of so they can see that it's not the answer."

Jim Carrey

There's a feeling that's hard to explain but deeply familiar to many: the desire to disappear. Not in a dramatic way, not always with tears or crisis—but quietly. You want to vanish from conversations, from responsibilities, from expectations. You want to stop being seen, stop being needed, stop being "on." You're not trying to end everything—you just want a break from being you.

This feeling often comes during emotional overload. When stress, loneliness, and self-doubt pile up, the mind searches for escape. And sometimes, disappearing feels like the only option. It's not about giving up—it's about wanting relief.

How It Feels

Wanting to disappear feels like:

Avoiding messages, because even replying feels too heavy.

Wanting silence, not just around you, but inside you.

Feeling like you're too much, and not enough at the same time.

Wishing you could pause life, without having to explain why.

Feeling invisible, and wondering if that would be easier.

It's the kind of emotional fatigue that makes you fantasize about being somewhere else, someone else, or nowhere at all. You don't want attention—you want absence.

Real-Life Examples

In social settings:

Mehak is at a family gathering. Everyone's talking, laughing, asking questions. She smiles, nods, plays along. But inside, she's overwhelmed. She wishes she could slip away unnoticed, just for a while.

At work:

Ravi is buried in deadlines. His inbox is full, his calendar packed. He feels like he's failing, even though he's trying. He fantasizes about quitting, disappearing, starting over somewhere no one knows him.

In relationships:

Aarav feels emotionally drained. He loves his partner, but the weight of communication, expectations, and emotional labor feels too much. He doesn't want to leave—he just wants to disappear for a day, a week, a breath.

In daily life:

Sunita wakes up and feels the heaviness before her feet touch the floor. She goes through the motions, but inside, she's numb. She wishes she could vanish—no responsibilities, no conversations, no pretending.

A Principle to Rise: The Principle of Gentle Reconnection

When the desire to disappear takes hold, the answer isn't to force yourself back–it's to reconnect gently. This is the Principle of Gentle Reconnection.

Gentle Reconnection means:

Honor the feeling without shame: Wanting to disappear doesn't make you weak–it means you're overwhelmed. Acknowledge it with compassion.

Create intentional space: Take a break. Log off. Step away. But do it with care, not guilt. You're allowed to rest.

Reconnect with yourself first: Before returning to others, return to you. Journal. Walk. Breathe. Ask, "What do I need right now?"

Choose one small point of contact: Send one message. Share one truth. Let someone know you're here, even if you're quiet.

Let go of performance: You don't have to be cheerful, productive, or perfect. You just have to be present.

Build back slowly: Reconnection isn't a leap–it's a series of gentle steps. One moment, one breath, one choice at a time.

Gentle reconnection is the quiet act of returning–not because you're forced to, but because you're ready. It's the reminder that disappearing isn't the end–it's a signal. And you can listen to it, honor it, and still find your way back.

Part Three

Emotions We Hide

Chapter 1
Loneliness in a Crowded Room

You're surrounded by people—talking, laughing, moving through life. The room is full, but your heart feels empty. You smile, nod, maybe even join the conversation, but inside, there's a quiet ache. You feel disconnected, unseen, and strangely alone. This is loneliness in a crowded room—a paradox that many experience but few talk about.

It's not about being physically alone. It's about feeling emotionally isolated, even when you're in the middle of a group. You might be at a party, in a meeting, at a family gathering, or scrolling through social media—and still feel like you don't belong. You're present, but not connected.

How It Feels

Loneliness in a crowded room feels like:

Being surrounded by noise, but feeling unheard.

Smiling on the outside, while feeling invisible inside.

Feeling like an outsider, even among familiar faces.

Wanting to leave, not because you dislike the people—but because you feel emotionally absent.

Feeling emotionally exhausted, from pretending to be okay.

It's the kind of loneliness that's hard to explain. You're not isolated in space—you're isolated in spirit.

Real-Life Examples

At a family gathering:

Mehak sits at the dinner table, surrounded by relatives. Everyone's talking and laughing, but no one asks how she's really doing. She feels like a guest in her own family, smiling to avoid questions.

At work:

Ravi attends a team meeting. Ideas are exchanged, jokes are made. He contributes, but feels disconnected. No one notices his silence between tasks. He wonders if anyone would notice if he stopped showing up.

In friendships:

Aarav goes out with friends. They talk about their lives, their plans, their relationships. He listens, nods, laughs—but doesn't share his own struggles. He feels like he's there physically, but emotionally absent.

On social media:

Sunita scrolls through her feed, seeing people living, celebrating, connecting. She feels like she's watching life from behind glass—present, but not part of it.

A Principle to Rise: The Principle of Intentional Connection

To heal loneliness in a crowded room, you don't need more people—you need more presence. This is the Principle of Intentional Connection.

Intentional Connection means:

Seek depth, not quantity: One meaningful conversation can be more healing than a hundred surface-level interactions.

Share your truth in safe spaces: Choose one person and say, "I've been feeling disconnected lately." Vulnerability invites closeness.

Ask for emotional presence: Let people know you need more than company—you need connection. It's okay to ask.

Be present yourself: Put down your phone. Listen fully. Engage with curiosity. Presence is a two-way street.

Create moments of realness: Instead of small talk, ask deeper questions. "What's been on your mind lately?" "What's something you've been carrying?"

Reconnect with yourself first: Loneliness often begins within. Journal, reflect, and ask, "What do I need to feel seen?"

Intentional connection is the quiet courage to say, "I want to be known." It's the shift from blending in to showing up. And it's the reminder that even in a crowded room, you deserve to feel like you belong.

Chapter 2
Anger You Can't Explain

"When I do not succeed I get mad with anger."

Simone de Beauvoir

There's a kind of anger that doesn't come with shouting or slamming doors. It simmers quietly beneath the surface. It shows up in irritability, in snapping at small things, in feeling overwhelmed by everyday tasks. You don't know exactly why you're angry–you just know you are. And that confusion makes it harder to talk about, harder to release, and harder to heal.

This is anger you can't explain–the kind that's rooted not in one event, but in a buildup of stress, unmet needs, emotional exhaustion, and unspoken pain. It's the kind of anger that feels unjustified, so you push it down. But suppressed anger doesn't disappear–it leaks into your relationships, your self-talk, and your body.

How It Feels

Unexplained anger feels like:

Being easily irritated, even by things that normally wouldn't bother you.

Feeling emotionally heavy, but not knowing why.

Snapping at loved ones, then feeling guilty afterward.

Wanting space, but not knowing how to ask for it.

Feeling misunderstood, even when you haven't said anything.

It's the kind of emotion that makes you feel like you're walking around with a storm inside—one you don't fully understand, and one you're afraid to let out.

Real-Life Examples

At home:

Mehak finds herself getting angry when her sibling asks a simple question. She responds sharply, then immediately regrets it. She doesn't know why she's so reactive—she just feels overwhelmed.

At work:

Ravi feels irritated by every email, every meeting, every request. He's not angry at anyone in particular, but the constant pressure makes him feel like he's on edge all the time.

In relationships:

Aarav loves his partner, but lately, he's been short-tempered. Small disagreements turn into big arguments. He doesn't know why he's so reactive—he just feels like he's carrying too much.

In daily life:

Sunita feels angry when she sees happy posts on social media. She doesn't want to feel bitter, but something inside her aches. She realizes she's been suppressing her own sadness for too long.

A Principle to Rise: The Principle of Emotional Mapping

To understand and release unexplained anger, you don't need to justify it–you need to map it. This is the Principle of Emotional Mapping.

Emotional Mapping means:

Pause and name the feeling: When anger arises, ask, "What am I really feeling?" Often, anger is a mask for hurt, fear, or fatigue.

Trace the trigger: Reflect on recent events. What's been building up? What needs have gone unmet? What boundaries have been crossed?

Write it out: Journaling helps externalize the emotion. Write without judgment. Let the anger speak.

Release through movement: Anger lives in the body. Walk, stretch, dance, or punch a pillow. Let your body help you process.

Communicate with clarity: When you're ready, express your feelings to someone you trust. Say, "I've been feeling off, and I think it's coming out as anger."

Practice self-compassion: You're not wrong for feeling angry. You're human. Treat yourself with the same kindness you'd offer a friend.

Emotional mapping is the gentle process of turning confusion into clarity. It's the reminder that anger isn't the enemy–it's a signal. And when you listen to it with compassion, it can lead you back to peace.

Chapter 3
Guilt That Lingers

"Every man is guilty of all the good he did not do."

Voltaire

Guilt is a natural emotion. It's meant to guide us, to help us reflect, to encourage repair. But sometimes, guilt doesn't pass–it stays. It lingers in the background of your thoughts, quietly shaping how you see yourself. You've apologized, you've tried to move on, but the feeling remains. It's not just about what you did–it becomes about who you are.

Lingering guilt is often tied to unresolved emotions, unmet forgiveness, or internalized shame. It's the kind of guilt that doesn't need reminders–you carry it with you. And over time, it can turn into self-punishment, keeping you stuck in a cycle of regret and self-doubt.

How It Feels

Lingering guilt feels like:

Replaying the same moment, wondering what you could've done differently.

Feeling undeserving of happiness, because you believe you haven't "earned" it.

Avoiding certain people or places, because they remind you of what happened.

Over-apologizing, even for things that aren't your fault.

Feeling like you're still paying for a mistake, long after it's passed.

It's the kind of emotion that quietly erodes your self-worth. You don't just feel bad about what happened—you start to feel bad about yourself.

Real-Life Examples

In relationships:

Mehak ended a friendship abruptly during a stressful time. Years later, she still feels guilty. She wonders if she should reach out, but fears rejection. She carries the guilt silently, unsure how to let it go.

At work:

Ravi missed a deadline that affected his team. He apologized, and the team moved on—but he didn't. He still feels like he let everyone down. Every new task feels like a test to prove he's not a failure.

In parenting:

Sunita lost her temper with her child during a tough week. She apologized, hugged them, and tried to make it right. But the guilt lingers. She questions her ability to be a good mother, even though her child has forgiven her.

In personal choices:

Aarav chose to prioritize his mental health and left a demanding job. He knows it was the right decision, but he feels guilty for leaving his team behind. He wonders if he was selfish, even though he was struggling.

A Principle to Rise: The Principle of Compassionate Accountability

To release lingering guilt, you don't need to forget—you need to forgive and integrate. This is the Principle of Compassionate Accountability.

Compassionate Accountability means:

Acknowledge the guilt without judgment: Say, "I feel guilty because I care." Guilt is a sign of conscience, not condemnation.

Separate guilt from shame: Guilt says, "I did something wrong." Shame says, "I am wrong." Don't confuse the two.

Make amends where possible: If you can apologize or repair—do it. If not, write a letter you don't send. Closure can be internal.

Learn from the experience: Ask, "What did this teach me?" Let guilt become growth, not punishment.

Practice self-forgiveness: Say, "I made a mistake, but I'm still worthy." Repeat it until it feels true.

Release through ritual: Write the guilt down and burn the paper. Speak it aloud and let it go. Symbolic release helps emotional healing.

Compassionate accountability is the balance between owning your actions and honoring your humanity. It's the reminder that you can be responsible and kind to yourself. That you can grow from guilt—without being defined by it.

Chapter 4
Grief That Doesn't Follow Rules

"You don't go around grief–you go through it."

Megan Devine (Grief therapist and author)

"Grief and healing can coexist."

David Kessler (Grief expert)

Grief is often portrayed as a linear process–stages you move through, milestones you reach, closure you eventually find. But real grief doesn't follow rules. It doesn't arrive on schedule, behave predictably, or fade neatly with time. It's messy, personal, and often misunderstood. It can show up years later, in unexpected moments, in places you thought were safe.

Unstructured grief is the kind that lingers quietly. It doesn't always come with tears or dramatic breakdowns. Sometimes, it's a dull ache. Sometimes, it's anger. Sometimes, it's numbness. And sometimes, it's confusion–because you don't even know why you're grieving, or why it still hurts.

How It Feels

Grief that doesn't follow rules feels like:

Sudden waves of sadness, even when life seems "normal."

Feeling guilty for still grieving, as if you should've "moved on" by now.

Struggling to explain your emotions, because they don't fit a clear narrative.

Feeling disconnected from others, because they expect you to be okay.

Experiencing joy and grief at the same time, and not knowing how to hold both.

It's the kind of emotion that doesn't ask for permission. It just shows up—and stays as long as it needs to.

Real-Life Examples

After a loss:

Mehak lost her father three years ago. She thought she had processed it. But one day, while watching a movie, she breaks down. The grief feels fresh again. She wonders why it's resurfacing now, and whether she's healing "wrong."

In daily life:

Ravi moved cities for a new job. He left behind friends, routines, and familiarity. He didn't expect to grieve the change—but he does. He feels lonely, nostalgic, and unsure how to talk about it, because it wasn't a "big" loss.

In relationships:

Aarav ended a long-term relationship. He knows it was the right decision, but months later, he still feels grief. Not just for the person, but for the version of himself that existed in that relationship. He misses the comfort, even while embracing the growth.

In identity shifts:

Sunita became a mother and loves her child deeply. But she grieves her old life—her freedom, her spontaneity, her sense of self. She feels guilty for feeling this way, but the grief is real, even if it's not about death.

A Principle to Rise: The Principle of Permission to Feel

To navigate grief that doesn't follow rules, you don't need to fix it—you need to honor it. This is the Principle of Permission to Feel.

Permission to Feel means:

Let go of timelines: Healing doesn't follow a calendar. You're allowed to grieve for as long as you need.

Name your grief: Say, "I'm grieving..." even if it's not a person. Grief can be for places, phases, dreams, or identities.

Feel without justification: You don't need a reason to feel sad. Emotions are valid, even when they're inconvenient.

Create space for expression: Journal, cry, talk, walk—whatever helps you release. Expression is part of healing.

Accept emotional contradictions: You can feel joy and grief at the same time. Let both exist without guilt.

Seek support without shame: Talk to someone who won't rush your healing. You deserve to be held, not hurried.

Permission to feel is the quiet strength to say, "I'm grieving, and that's okay." It's the reminder that healing isn't about getting over—it's about learning to live with love, loss, and everything in between.

Chapter 5
Feeling Numb

"The body shuts down when it has too much to bear; goes its own way quietly inside, waiting for a better time, leaving you numb and half alive."

Jeanette Winterson

There's a kind of emotional silence that doesn't scream–it just settles in. You're not sad, not angry, not joyful. You're just... blank. You go through the motions, respond when needed, smile when expected–but inside, there's nothing. This is numbness–a hidden emotion that often follows prolonged stress, grief, or emotional overload.

Feeling numb isn't the absence of emotion–it's the mind's way of protecting itself when emotions become too much. It's a survival response, not a failure. But when numbness lingers, it can feel like you're disconnected from life, from others, and from yourself.

How It Feels

Emotional numbness feels like:

Going through the motions, without feeling connected to what you're doing.

Not reacting to things that used to matter, even things you love.

Feeling distant from people, even those closest to you.

Struggling to cry or feel joy, even when you want to.

Wondering what's wrong with you, because you feel nothing.

It's the kind of state where everything feels muted. You're not drowning—but you're not breathing deeply either. You're just floating.

Real-Life Examples

In daily life:

Mehak wakes up, makes breakfast, goes to work, comes home. She does everything she's supposed to, but it all feels flat. She used to enjoy music, books, and long walks. Now, she feels indifferent. She wonders if she's broken.

At work:

Ravi used to feel proud of his accomplishments. Now, even when he finishes a big project, he feels nothing. He's not unhappy—he's just disconnected. He starts questioning whether anything he does really matters.

In relationships:

Aarav loves his partner, but lately, he feels emotionally distant. He listens, responds, and shows up—but he doesn't feel present. He's not angry or upset—he just feels blank. And he doesn't know how to explain it.

After loss:

Sunita lost her mother six months ago. She cried a lot in the beginning, but now she feels nothing. People assume she's healed, but she feels frozen. She wants to feel again—but doesn't know how.

A Principle to Rise: The Principle of Gentle Awakening

To move through numbness, you don't need to force emotion–you need to invite it back slowly. This is the Principle of Gentle Awakening.

Gentle Awakening means:

Accept the numbness without judgment: Say, "This is how I feel right now." Numbness is not failure–it's a signal.

Reconnect through the senses: Touch, taste, sound, movement–engage with the physical world to gently stir emotion.

Create small moments of meaning: Watch a sunset. Listen to a favorite song. Write a few honest lines. Let life in, one moment at a time.

Avoid emotional pressure: Don't force yourself to feel. Instead, create space where feelings are welcome, not demanded.

Talk about the numbness: Share with someone you trust. Say, "I don't feel much lately, and I don't know why." Speaking it aloud can soften the silence.

Be patient with your healing: Emotions return in layers. Trust that feeling will come back–not all at once, but in time.

Gentle awakening is the quiet process of returning to yourself. It's the reminder that numbness is not the end–it's a pause. And with care, presence, and patience, you can begin to feel again.

Chapter 6
Crying Without Knowing Why

"If somebody hurts you, it's okay to cry a river.
Just remember to build a bridge and get over it."

Taylor Swift

"Tears are the silent language of grief and healing.
Embrace them as part of your journey."

Jeremiah Say

There are moments when tears come without warning. You're not watching a sad movie. Nothing tragic has happened. You're just sitting at your desk, walking down the street, or folding laundry–and suddenly, your eyes well up. You wipe them away quickly, confused. You ask yourself, "Why am I crying?" but no answer comes.

This kind of crying doesn't always have a clear reason. It's not about one big thing–it's about everything. It's the weight of unspoken emotions, the quiet build-up of stress, the loneliness you've been ignoring. It's your body speaking when your mind has gone silent.

How It Feels

Crying without knowing why feels like:

A sudden wave of emotion that catches you off guard.

A heaviness in your chest that you didn't realize was there.

Feeling emotionally full, like you've been carrying too much for too long.

A sense of confusion—because nothing "bad" happened, but something still hurts.

A quiet kind of sadness that doesn't have a name.

It's not dramatic. It's not loud. It's a soft unraveling. And it often happens when you finally slow down—when the noise fades and your emotions have space to surface.

Real-Life Examples

The Quiet Breakdown:

Ishu is doing the dishes after dinner. It's been a long day, but nothing unusual. Suddenly, she starts crying. She doesn't know why. But deep down, it's the exhaustion of always being "okay," of holding everything together without a break.

The Commute Cry:

Karan is on the metro, headphones in, staring out the window. A song plays, and tears start to fall. He's not heartbroken. He's not sad about anything specific. But the loneliness of a new city, the pressure of work, and the absence of real connection have all piled up quietly.

The Unexpected Trigger:

Ananya sees a childhood photo while scrolling through her gallery. She tears up. Not because of the photo itself, but because it reminds her of a time when life felt simpler, safer. The contrast to her current emotional state hits her harder than she expected.

The Accumulated Stress:

Alex has been pushing through deadlines, skipping meals, and ignoring his feelings. One night, while brushing his teeth, he breaks down. It's not about that moment–it's about all the moments he didn't allow himself to feel.

A Principle to Rise: The Principle of Emotional Check-In

Crying without knowing why is often a sign that you've been emotionally disconnected from yourself. The way to rise is not to stop the tears–but to listen to them. This is the Principle of Emotional Check-In.

Emotional Check-In means:

Pause and Acknowledge:

When tears come, don't rush to stop them. Say to yourself, "Something inside me needs attention." This creates space for compassion instead of confusion.

Name the Feeling:

Try to identify what you're feeling. Even if it's vague–lonely, tired, overwhelmed–naming it helps you understand it.

Trace the Source:

Ask, "What's been building up lately?" It might not be one big thing. It might be a series of small things you've been carrying silently.

Allow the Release:

Let yourself cry. Write. Talk to someone. Crying is not weakness–it's a release valve for emotions that have nowhere else to go.

Refill Your Emotional Tank:

After the release, do something nurturing. Rest. Walk. Listen to music. You've emptied something–now refill it with care.

This principle isn't just for when you cry. It's a daily practice. A few minutes each day to ask yourself, "How am I really feeling?" can prevent emotional overflow later. It's not about fixing everything–it's about staying connected to yourself.

Chapter 7
The Ache of Rejection

"Success is buried on the other side of rejection."

Tony Robbins

"If we live for people's acceptance, we will die from their rejection."

Lecrae

"I take rejection as someone blowing a bugle in my ear to wake me up and get going, rather than retreat."

Sylvester Stallone

"Rejection is a big part of show business. It can be tough on anyone who doesn't have fairly good self-esteem."

Angela Cartwright

Rejection doesn't always come with a loud "no." Sometimes, it's a silence that lingers after you've reached out. A message that goes unanswered. A job application that disappears into a void. A friend who slowly drifts away. It's subtle, but it stings.

Rejection isn't just about being turned down—it's about feeling unwanted, unseen, or not enough. It's the ache that settles in your chest when someone chooses not to choose you. And it's one of the deepest ways stress, negativity, and loneliness show up in everyday life.

How It Feels

The ache of rejection feels like:

A sharp drop in self-worth, even if you were feeling confident moments before.

Questioning your value, your appearance, your words—everything.

Feeling exposed, like you took a risk and now regret it.

A quiet sadness that follows you around, even when you're trying to stay busy.

Wanting to withdraw, to protect yourself from future hurt.

It's not just about the moment of rejection—it's about what it awakens. Old insecurities. Past wounds. The fear that maybe you're not good enough, and never will be.

Real-Life Examples

Romantic Rejection:

Aditi finally tells someone she likes them. They respond kindly, but say they don't feel the same. She smiles and says, "It's okay," but later, she cries alone. It's not just about them—it's about feeling unlovable.

Professional Rejection:

Rohit applies for a job he really wants. He prepares, interviews, and waits. Then comes the email: "We've decided to move forward with another candidate." He tells himself it's fine, but inside, he feels like a failure.

Social Rejection:

Neha invites friends to a gathering. Only two show up. The rest cancel or don't respond. She laughs it off, but later wonders, "Do people even want to be around me?"

Family Rejection:

Arjun opens up to his parents about his career struggles. They dismiss it, saying, "You just need to work harder." He feels unheard, unsupported, and alone—even in his own home.

A Principle to Rise: The Principle of Inner Reaffirmation

Rejection hurts because it touches the part of us that seeks connection and validation. The way to rise is not to avoid rejection—but to build a stronger relationship with yourself. This is the Principle of Inner Reaffirmation.

Inner Reaffirmation means:

Separate the event from your identity:

Rejection is an experience, not a definition. You weren't rejected because you're unworthy—you were rejected because something didn't align. That's all.

Affirm your value actively:

After rejection, say to yourself: "I am still valuable. I am still enough." Repeat it until it feels true again. Your worth doesn't depend on someone else's approval.

Reflect, don't ruminate:

Ask: "Is there something I can learn from this?" If yes, take the lesson. If not, let it go. Don't turn rejection into a personal attack.

Reconnect with what makes you whole:

Do something that reminds you of your strengths—write, create, help someone, revisit a past success. These are reminders that you are more than this moment.

Stay open, even when it hurts:

Rejection tempts us to shut down. But healing comes from staying open—to new people, new chances, and new ways of being seen.

This principle isn't just for big rejections. It's for the small ones too—the unanswered texts, the missed invitations, the quiet dismissals. Every time you feel unwanted, come back to yourself. Reaffirm your worth. You are not defined by who walks away—you are defined by how you rise.

Chapter 8
The Pain of Not Being Seen

"The thing that I'm most worried about is just being alone without anybody to care for or someone who will care for me."

Anne Hathaway

"Being noticed can be a burden... So I disappear a lot."

Bob Dylan

There's a kind of loneliness that doesn't come from being alone–it comes from being surrounded by people who don't truly see you. You show up, you speak, you try–but it feels like you're invisible. Your efforts go unnoticed. Your emotions go unacknowledged. Your presence feels like background noise.

Not being seen isn't just about attention–it's about recognition. It's the human need to be understood, valued, and acknowledged. And when that need isn't met, it creates a quiet pain that lingers beneath the surface.

How It Feels

The pain of not being seen feels like:

Speaking in a room and realizing no one is really listening.

Sharing something personal and getting a generic response.

Being praised for things that don't reflect who you truly are.

Feeling like you have to perform or pretend just to be accepted.

Wondering if anyone would notice if you stopped showing up.

It's subtle. It's silent. But it's heavy. It makes you question your worth, your place, and your voice. And over time, it can lead to emotional exhaustion and deep loneliness–even in the middle of a crowd.

Real-Life Examples

In Friendships:

Tanya always supports her friends–she listens, shows up, and remembers the little things. But when she's going through something, no one asks how she's doing. She feels like a giver, not a person. Like her feelings don't matter.

At Work:

Vikram works hard, stays late, and brings creative ideas. But in meetings, his contributions are overlooked. Others get credit. He starts to feel invisible, like his presence is just expected, not appreciated.

In Family:

Rhea tries to express her dreams to her parents. They nod, but quickly change the topic to something "more practical." She feels dismissed, like her inner world doesn't matter. Like she's only seen for what she does, not who she is.

In Relationships:

Aman feels emotionally disconnected from his partner. He shares his thoughts, but they're met with silence or indifference. He begins to wonder if he's truly known–or just tolerated.

A Principle to Rise: The Principle of Self-Visibility

When others don't see you, it's easy to shrink. To become quieter, smaller, less expressive. But the way to rise is not to wait for others to notice–it's to start seeing yourself. This is the Principle of Self-Visibility.

Self-Visibility means:

Validate your own presence:

Remind yourself: "I matter. My thoughts, feelings, and experiences are real." You don't need external proof to exist fully.

Express yourself authentically:

Speak your truth, even if it's not received perfectly. The more you show up as yourself, the more visible you become–to yourself and others.

Create spaces where you're seen:

Seek out relationships, communities, and environments where you feel acknowledged. Don't settle for places that dim your light.

Document your inner world:

Journal, create, reflect. Let your emotions live somewhere. Even if no one else sees them, you do–and that matters.

Be your own witness:

Celebrate your growth, your efforts, your resilience. Notice yourself. Applaud yourself. You are worthy of recognition–even if it starts with you.

This principle isn't about ignoring the pain–it's about transforming it. When you begin to see yourself clearly, you stop depending on others to define your worth. You become your own mirror, your own witness, your own source of light.

Chapter 9
Emotional Exhaustion

People cry, not because they're weak.
It's because they've been strong for too long."

Johnny Depp

"When I'm tired, I rest. I say, 'I can't be a superwoman today."

Jada Pinkett Smith

"If you feel 'burnout' setting in, if you feel demoralized and exhausted, it is best, for the sake of everyone, to withdraw and restore yourself."

Dalai Lama

There's a kind of tiredness that sleep doesn't fix. You wake up feeling drained. You go through the day on autopilot. You smile, respond, perform—but inside, you feel empty. It's not just physical fatigue. It's emotional exhaustion.

Emotional exhaustion happens when you've been carrying too much for too long—stress, responsibilities, unresolved emotions, constant pressure to be "okay." It's the burnout of the heart. And it's one of the most silent ways negativity, stress, and loneliness show up in everyday life.

How It Feels

Emotional exhaustion feels like:

Waking up tired, even after a full night's sleep.

Feeling numb—like you've stopped caring, even about things that used to matter.

Struggling to make decisions, because everything feels overwhelming.

Wanting to be alone, not because you enjoy solitude, but because you have nothing left to give.

Feeling like you're surviving, not living.

It's not always dramatic. Sometimes, it's just a slow fading of energy, motivation, and joy. You keep going, but you're running on empty.

Real-Life Examples

Work Burnout:

Sneha works long hours, meets deadlines, and handles team conflicts. She's praised for being reliable. But lately, she feels disconnected. She stares at her screen, unable to focus. She's not lazy—she's emotionally depleted.

Caregiver Fatigue:

Ramesh takes care of his aging parents while managing his own family. He doesn't complain. But one day, he breaks down while making tea. It's not the tea—it's the months of emotional labor without rest or recognition.

Relationship Drain:

Ishita is always the emotional anchor in her relationship. She listens, supports, and forgives. But she feels unseen. Her emotional tank is empty, and she starts withdrawing—not out of anger, but out of exhaustion.

Social Overload:

Aarav attends every event, replies to every message, and tries to be there for everyone. But he feels hollow. He's surrounded by people, yet feels completely alone. His emotional bandwidth is gone.

A Principle to Rise: The Principle of Emotional Refueling

Emotional exhaustion isn't solved by pushing through—it's healed by refueling. The way to rise is to stop pouring from an empty cup and start filling it again. This is the Principle of Emotional Refueling.

Emotional Refueling means:

Recognize the signs early:

Don't wait until you break down. Notice when you start feeling numb, irritable, or disconnected. These are signals—not flaws.

Give yourself permission to rest:

Rest isn't laziness. It's recovery. Take breaks, cancel plans, say no. You're allowed to protect your energy.

Engage in restorative activities:

Do things that nourish you emotionally—reading, walking, music, silence. Not everything has to be productive. Some things just need to be peaceful.

Set emotional boundaries:

You don't have to be available to everyone all the time. Protect your space. Say, "I need time for myself." That's not selfish—it's survival.

Reconnect with joy:

Exhaustion dims joy. So actively seek it. Watch something funny. Dance. Laugh. Play. These moments refill what stress drains.

This principle isn't about fixing everything overnight. It's about creating a rhythm of emotional care. When you start refueling regularly, you stop running on empty. You begin to feel again. To live again. To rise again.

Chapter 10
The Fear of Vulnerability

"Love comes when manipulation stops; when you think more about the other person than about his or her reactions to you. When you dare to reveal yourself fully. When you dare to be vulnerable."

Joyce Brothers

"What happens when people open their hearts? They get better."

Haruki Murakami

There's a moment–just before you open up–when your heart races. You want to say how you really feel, but something holds you back. You hesitate. You edit your words. You smile instead. Because being vulnerable feels risky. It feels like handing someone a fragile part of you and hoping they won't drop it.

Vulnerability isn't weakness–it's honesty. It's the courage to be seen, to be real, to be human. But for many, it's terrifying. Because when you've been hurt before, opening up feels like inviting pain in again. And so, you hide. You protect. You pretend. And in doing so, you slowly disconnect from others–and from yourself.

Beyond our thoughts, dreams, and identities, we are physical beings–made of flesh and emotion. We can be hurt deeply, both physically and emotionally, and those wounds may not heal easily, but healing is always possible.

How It Feels

The fear of vulnerability feels like:

Wanting to cry, but holding it in because you don't want to seem "too emotional."

Having something important to say, but staying silent out of fear of judgment.

Feeling lonely, but pretending you're fine because asking for support feels too exposed.

Laughing things off that actually hurt, just to avoid seeming "dramatic."

Keeping your guard up, even with people who care about you.

It's exhausting. It's isolating. And it often comes from a place of self-protection–because somewhere along the way, being open led to being hurt.

Real-Life Examples

In Friendships:

Jasanpreet is going through a tough time, but when her friends ask how she's doing, she says, "I'm okay." She wants to talk, but she's afraid they'll think she's too much. So she keeps it light–and feels even more alone.

At Work:

Rahul has a new idea, but he's afraid of being criticized. So he stays quiet in meetings. He watches others speak up and get noticed, while he hides behind his fear of being wrong.

In Relationships:

Simran wants to tell her partner that she feels distant, but she's scared it'll start a fight. So she says nothing. The silence grows. The distance deepens. And the relationship suffers–not from conflict, but from avoidance.

In Family:

Nandini wants to tell his parents he's struggling with anxiety. But he fears they won't understand. So he smiles, performs, and keeps the truth buried. Inside, he feels like no one really knows him.

A Principle to Rise: The Principle of Safe Expression

The fear of vulnerability doesn't go away by force–it softens through safety. The way to rise is not to expose everything at once, but to create spaces where your truth can breathe. This is the Principle of Safe Expression.

Safe Expression means:

Start small, but start real:

You don't have to share everything. Begin with one honest sentence. One truth. One feeling. Vulnerability grows with practice.

Choose your audience wisely:

Not everyone deserves your deepest truths. Share with those who've earned your trust. Vulnerability is a gift–give it where it's safe.

Validate your own emotions first:

Before you open up to others, remind yourself: "What I feel is valid. I don't need to justify it." This builds inner confidence.

Use "I" language:

Say, "I feel hurt," instead of "You hurt me." This keeps the focus on your experience and reduces defensiveness in others.

Celebrate your courage:

Every time you express something real, acknowledge it. Vulnerability isn't easy—but it's powerful. It's how connection begins.

This principle isn't about being open with everyone—it's about being honest with yourself, and slowly with others. When you allow yourself to be seen, you give others permission to do the same. And in that space, healing begins.

Part four

The Shift Begins

Chapter 1
Naming What Hurts

"I don't know if there is any specific way to handle emotional pain. Loved ones, music, and self-medicating seem to help me."

Mpho Koaho

"The wound is where the light enters you."

Rumi

Healing doesn't begin with fixing–it begins with naming. Before you can rise from pain, you have to recognize it. Not just feel it vaguely, but call it what it is. "I'm hurt because I felt ignored." "I'm angry because I was betrayed." "I'm scared because I don't feel safe." These are not just words–they are keys. Because when you name what hurts, you stop running from it. You start facing it.

Most people carry pain they haven't named. They feel anxious, but don't know why. They feel heavy, but can't explain it. So they distract themselves, bury the feeling, or pretend it's not there. But unnamed pain doesn't disappear–it grows. It shows up in stress, in relationships, in loneliness. Naming it is the first shift toward healing.

How It Feels

Not naming what hurts feels like:

Carrying a weight you can't describe, but still feel every day.

Feeling triggered by small things, without knowing why.

Avoiding silence, because it brings up emotions you don't want to face.

Feeling disconnected from yourself, like you're living on the surface.

Numbing out–through work, entertainment, or busyness–because naming the pain feels too vulnerable.

It's like walking around with a wound you haven't looked at. You feel it, but you don't treat it. And over time, it shapes how you see yourself, others, and the world.

Real-Life Examples

Unspoken Grief:

Meera lost her father two years ago. She never talked about it. She went back to work, smiled through the days, and told herself she was "strong." But she feels emotionally distant, and doesn't know why. The grief is still there–unnamed, unprocessed.

Hidden Insecurity:

Ravi always feels anxious in social settings. He thinks he's just "shy," but deep down, he fears rejection. He was bullied in school, and never named that pain. Now, every interaction feels like a test he's afraid to fail.

Buried Anger:

Aarushi constantly feels irritated with her partner. She snaps over small things. But the real hurt is from years of feeling unheard. She never said, "I feel invisible." So the anger keeps leaking out in other ways.

Unacknowledged Fear:

Karan avoids commitment. He tells people he's "just not ready." But the truth is, he's scared of being abandoned. His parents' divorce left a mark he never named. So he keeps relationships shallow—to protect himself from a pain he hasn't faced.

A Principle to Rise: The Principle of Honest Labeling

You can't heal what you won't name. The way to rise is to stop hiding your pain behind vague feelings and start calling it what it is. This is the Principle of Honest Labeling.

Honest Labeling means:

Pause and ask:

When you feel off, ask yourself: "What exactly hurts?" Don't settle for "I'm fine" or "I'm just tired." Dig deeper.

Use clear emotional language:

Say, "I feel rejected," instead of "I'm upset." Say, "I feel unsafe," instead of "I'm just stressed." The more specific, the more powerful.

Write it down:

Journaling helps you name what's swirling inside. Even one sentence like "I feel hurt because..." can unlock clarity.

Speak it aloud (when safe):

Share your truth with someone you trust. Naming pain out loud makes it real—and real things can be healed.

Validate your own experience:

Don't judge your emotions. Don't compare your pain. If it hurts, it matters. Naming it is not weakness—it's strength.

This principle is the beginning of the shift. When you name what hurts, you stop being controlled by it. You start understanding it, working with it, and eventually—rising above it.

Chapter 2
Learning to Sit With Discomfort

"Lean into the discomfort of the work."

Brené Brown

"The more time you spend in your discomfort zone,
the more your comfort zone will expand."

Robin Sharma

We're taught to escape discomfort. Distract yourself. Fix it. Avoid it. Numb it. But healing doesn't happen in avoidance—it happens in presence. Discomfort isn't the enemy. It's a messenger. It shows up when something needs attention, when something is shifting, when something is asking to be felt.

Learning to sit with discomfort is one of the most powerful shifts in rising from negativity, stress, and loneliness. It's not about liking the pain–it's about allowing it. Because when you stop running from what hurts, you start understanding it. And that's where transformation begins.

How It Feels

Sitting with discomfort feels like:

Wanting to escape your own thoughts, but choosing to stay.

Feeling restless, anxious, or emotionally raw—and not numbing it.

Facing truths you've avoided, even when they make you uncomfortable.

Letting emotions rise without trying to control or suppress them.

Feeling exposed, uncertain, or vulnerable—but staying present anyway.

It's not easy. It's not comfortable. But it's honest. And honesty is the foundation of healing.

Real-Life Examples

Emotional Processing:

Priya feels anxious every evening. She usually scrolls through social media to distract herself. But one night, she puts her phone down and just sits. She feels the tightness in her chest, the racing thoughts. She breathes through it. It's hard—but she finally starts to understand what's beneath the anxiety.

Facing Loneliness:

Ravi spends weekends alone. He used to fill the silence with noise—TV, calls, errands. But now, he sits with the loneliness. He feels the ache, the emptiness. And slowly, he begins to ask deeper questions: "What am I really missing?" "What do I need?"

Conflict Avoidance:

Aarushi has tension with her sibling. She usually avoids conversations that might lead to conflict. But this time, she sits with the discomfort of honesty. She speaks her truth, listens, and feels the awkwardness. It's not smooth—but it's real. And it opens the door to healing.

Grief and Loss:

Karan lost his pet recently. He keeps himself busy to avoid the sadness. But one evening, he sits with the grief. He cries. He remembers. He feels. And in that moment, the pain becomes less overwhelming–because he's no longer fighting it.

A Principle to Rise: The Principle of Emotional Sitting

Discomfort is not a problem to solve–it's a space to enter. The way to rise is to stop escaping and start engaging. This is the Principle of Emotional Sitting.

Emotional Sitting means:

Notice the urge to escape:

When discomfort arises, pause. Ask yourself: "What am I trying to avoid?" Awareness is the first step.

Create safe space for feeling:

Sit in silence. Breathe. Journal. Let the emotion rise. You don't have to fix it–just feel it.

Name the discomfort:

Say, "I feel anxious," or "I feel sad." Naming it helps you stay present with it, rather than overwhelmed by it.

Stay with it, gently:

Don't force yourself to dive deep all at once. Stay for a few minutes. Build tolerance. Discomfort becomes less scary when you face it gradually.

Reflect afterward:

Ask: "What did I learn from sitting with this?" Often, discomfort carries wisdom. It shows you what needs healing, what needs change, what needs care.

When you learn to sit with discomfort, you stop fearing your emotions. You start trusting yourself. And in that trust, the shift begins.

Chapter 3
Finding Safety in Yourself

"The ache for home lives in all of us. The safe place where we can go as we are and not be questioned."

Maya Angelou

"Safety is a basic human need. People with a sense of security and belonging are stabilized for learning, creating, innovating."

John Sweeney

There's a kind of safety we search for in others–someone to understand us, protect us, stay with us. But what happens when that safety isn't there? When people leave, misunderstand, or disappoint? That's when the real shift begins: learning to find safety not outside, but within.

Finding safety in yourself means becoming your own anchor. It's knowing that even when the world feels unstable, you can trust your own presence. It's not about being perfectly healed–it's about being consistently kind to yourself. When you feel safe inside, you stop chasing validation, fearing rejection, or collapsing under loneliness. You begin to rise.

How It Feels

Finding safety in yourself feels like:

Trusting your emotions, even when they're messy.

Knowing you can handle discomfort without falling apart.

Feeling grounded, even when others don't understand you.

Speaking your truth without needing approval.

Being alone without feeling abandoned.

It's quiet. It's steady. It's the feeling of coming home to yourself—again and again.

Real-Life Examples

After a Breakup:

Judy's relationship ends suddenly. She feels lost, like her emotional safety net has been ripped away. But instead of rushing into another relationship, she starts journaling, meditating, and spending time alone. Slowly, she begins to feel safe in her own company.

In a Toxic Workplace:

Ravi works in a high-pressure job where he's constantly criticized. He used to doubt himself. But now, he starts affirming his worth daily. He sets boundaries, speaks up, and reminds himself: "I am not defined by this environment." His inner safety becomes stronger than external chaos.

During Family Conflict:

Aarushi often feels judged by her family. She used to shrink, trying to please everyone. But now, she practices self-validation. She tells herself, "I am allowed to be different." She no longer seeks safety in their approval–she finds it in her own truth.

Facing Loneliness:

Karan lives alone in a new city. He misses familiar faces. But instead of numbing the loneliness, he starts building routines that make him feel secure–morning walks, cooking, reading. He learns that solitude doesn't have to be scary when you feel safe inside.

A Principle to Rise: The Principle of Inner Anchoring

Safety isn't just about who's around you–it's about how you hold yourself. The way to rise is to become your own safe space. This is the Principle of Inner Anchoring.

Inner Anchoring means:

Build emotional rituals:

Create daily habits that ground you–journaling, breathing exercises, affirmations. These become your emotional anchors.

Speak kindly to yourself:

Replace self-criticism with compassion. Say, "I'm doing my best," or "It's okay to feel this." Your inner voice should be your safest companion.

Set boundaries that protect your peace:

Say no when needed. Step away from toxic dynamics. Safety grows when you stop betraying yourself to please others.

Trust your ability to cope:

Remind yourself of past challenges you've survived. You are stronger than you think. Safety comes from knowing you can handle life.

Create a space that reflects you:

Your room, your routine, your choices–make them feel like home. Physical safety supports emotional safety.

This principle is a turning point. When you find safety in yourself, you stop depending on unstable sources. You become your own foundation. And from that place, you rise—not because the world is perfect, but because you are anchored.

Chapter 4
Letting Go of Control

"Nothing can drag you down if you're not holding on to it."

Tony Robbins

"We must be willing to let go of the life we have planned, so as to have the life that is waiting for us."

E.M. Forster

"Letting go doesn't mean that you don't care about someone anymore. It's just realizing that the only person you really have control over is yourself."

Deborah Reber

Control feels safe. It gives us the illusion that if we plan enough, predict enough, prepare enough–we can avoid pain. We try to control outcomes, people, emotions, even the future. But control is a heavy burden. It's exhausting. And the truth is, life doesn't always follow our script.

Letting go of control isn't about giving up–it's about trusting. Trusting that you can handle what comes. Trusting that uncertainty doesn't always mean danger. Trusting that sometimes, peace comes not from holding tighter, but from loosening your grip.

This shift is essential in rising from negativity, stress, and loneliness. Because control often comes from fear—and healing begins when fear is replaced with trust.

How It Feels

Letting go of control feels like:

Releasing the need to know what's next, and choosing to be present.

Accepting that you can't change others, only how you respond.

Feeling anxious at first, but slowly discovering peace in surrender.

Watching things unfold without trying to force them.

Trusting that even if things don't go your way, you'll be okay.

It's uncomfortable at first. You feel exposed, uncertain, vulnerable. But over time, it becomes freeing. You stop fighting life—and start flowing with it.

Real-Life Examples

In Relationships:

Bhoomika constantly worries about her partner's behavior. She checks their phone, overthinks every word, tries to control the dynamic. But it only creates tension. When she starts letting go—focusing on her own peace instead of their actions—she feels lighter, more grounded.

At Work:

Ravi wants every project to be perfect. He micromanages, overworks, and stresses over every detail. But burnout hits. He learns to delegate, trust his team, and accept imperfection. His productivity improves—and so does his mental health.

In Parenting:

Aarushi wants her child to succeed, so she plans every moment. But her child feels pressured. When Aarushi lets go–allowing space for mistakes and growth–their bond strengthens. Control is replaced by connection.

In Healing:

Karan wants to "fix" his emotions quickly. He reads, journals, meditates–but still feels stuck. Eventually, he stops trying to control the process. He allows himself to feel, rest, and heal slowly. That's when real progress begins.

A Principle to Rise: The Principle of Surrendered Strength

Letting go of control doesn't mean weakness–it means strength in surrender. The way to rise is to trust yourself, trust the process, and stop gripping so tightly. This is the Principle of Surrendered Strength.

Surrendered Strength means:

Identify what you can and can't control:

Ask yourself: "Is this mine to manage?" If not, release it. Focus only on what's within your power–your actions, your mindset, your choices.

Practice mindful detachment:

Observe situations without trying to fix them immediately. Let things unfold. Detachment isn't indifference–it's peace.

Use grounding techniques:

When anxiety rises, breathe deeply. Repeat affirmations like "I trust the process," or "I am safe even in uncertainty."

Accept imperfection:

Life isn't perfect. People aren't perfect. You aren't perfect. And that's okay. Let go of the need to control every outcome.

Lean into trust:

Trust your resilience. Trust that even if things go wrong, you'll find your way. Trust that life has its own rhythm—and you don't have to force it.

This principle is a turning point. When you let go of control, you make space for flow, for peace, for growth. You stop resisting life—and start rising with it.

Chapter 5
Rewriting Your Inner Story

*"The most important story we'll ever write in life is our own–
not with ink but with our daily choices."*

Richard Paul Evans

We all carry stories inside us. Stories about who we are, what we deserve, what we're capable of. Some of these stories are empowering. But many are not. They come from past pain, rejection, failure, or criticism. Over time, they become beliefs: "I'm not good enough." "I always mess things up." "People always leave."

These stories shape how we see ourselves–and how we live. They influence our choices, relationships, and even our dreams. But here's the truth: your inner story is not fixed. It can be rewritten. And rewriting it is one of the most powerful shifts in rising from negativity, stress, and loneliness.

How It Feels

Rewriting your inner story feels like:

Challenging the voice in your head that says you're not enough.

Feeling uncomfortable as you let go of old beliefs.

Discovering new possibilities where you once saw limitations.

Replacing shame with compassion, fear with courage.

Slowly becoming the version of yourself you've always hoped to be.

It's not instant. It's not easy. But it's transformative. Because when your inner story changes, everything else begins to shift.

Real-Life Examples

From Self-Doubt to Self-Worth:

Meera grew up being told she was "too sensitive." She internalized it as weakness. As an adult, she avoids expressing emotions. But through therapy and journaling, she starts rewriting her story: "My sensitivity is my strength." She begins to speak up, connect deeply, and feel proud of who she is.

From Failure to Growth:

Ravi was fired from a job years ago. Since then, he's believed he's not capable. Every new opportunity feels like a threat. But one day, he reframes the experience: "That job wasn't right for me. I've grown since then." He applies for a new role–and gets it.

From Abandonment to Independence:

Aarushi's partner left her suddenly. She told herself, "I'm not lovable." But over time, she starts rewriting: "I am worthy of love. Their leaving wasn't about my value." She begins to build a life rooted in self-respect, not fear.

From Shame to Acceptance:

Karan struggled with anxiety for years. He felt broken. But after joining a support group, he starts telling a new story: "I'm human. I'm healing. I'm not alone." That shift helps him open up, connect, and grow.

A Principle to Rise: The Principle of Narrative Renewal

Your inner story is powerful—but it's not permanent. The way to rise is to challenge the old narrative and write a new one. This is the Principle of Narrative Renewal.

Narrative Renewal means:

Identify the old story:

Ask yourself: "What story have I been telling myself?" Write it down. Be honest. This is the starting point.

Challenge its truth:

Ask: "Is this story based on facts or fear?" "Who gave me this belief—and do I still want it?" Questioning weakens its grip.

Write a new story:

Create affirmations or journal entries that reflect your growth. For example: "I am learning." "I am worthy." "I am allowed to change."

Repeat the new narrative daily:

Your brain believes what it hears often. Speak your new story out loud. Let it become your inner voice.

Live in alignment with the new story:

Take actions that reflect your rewritten beliefs. If your new story is "I am confident," start showing up that way—even in small ways.

This principle is a turning point. When you rewrite your inner story, you reclaim your power. You stop living in the shadow of old wounds—and start walking in the light of new truths.

Chapter 6
Building Emotional Boundaries

"You teach people how to treat you by what you allow, what you stop, and what you reinforce."

Tony Gaskins

Not every emotion you feel is yours to carry. Not every problem is yours to solve. Not every mood in the room is yours to absorb. But when you lack emotional boundaries, everything seeps in. You feel responsible for others' happiness, guilty for saying no, and overwhelmed by the weight of emotions that aren't even yours.

Emotional boundaries are not walls–they're filters. They help you stay connected without losing yourself. They protect your energy, your peace, and your emotional clarity. And building them is a vital shift in rising from stress, negativity, and loneliness.

How It Feels

Building emotional boundaries feels like:

Saying "no" without guilt.

Feeling empathy without absorbing someone else's pain.

Recognizing when you're emotionally overloaded–and stepping back.

Trusting that you can care for others without abandoning yourself.

Feeling lighter, clearer, and more in control of your emotional space.

At first, it feels unfamiliar—even selfish. But over time, it feels like freedom. You stop drowning in others' emotions and start breathing in your own.

Real-Life Examples

In Friendships:

Meera is the "go-to" friend. People vent to her, lean on her, and expect her to always be available. She listens, comforts, and gives—even when she's exhausted. But one day, she sets a boundary: "I care about you, but I need space tonight." It's hard—but she feels relief. She's learning to protect her emotional energy.

At Work:

Ravi's colleague constantly complains and dumps emotional stress on him. Ravi used to absorb it, feeling drained after every interaction. Now, he sets a boundary: "I'm here to help with work, but I can't be your emotional outlet every day." He feels more focused, less burdened.

In Family:

Aarushi's parents often guilt her into decisions. She used to comply, fearing conflict. But now, she says: "I respect your opinion, but I need to make this choice for myself." She feels empowered, even if it's uncomfortable.

In Relationships:

Karan's partner often projects their stress onto him. He used to take it personally. Now, he reminds himself: "Their mood is not my fault." He listens with compassion—but doesn't lose himself in their storm.

A Principle to Rise: The Principle of Emotional Filtering

You don't have to carry everything. The way to rise is to filter what enters your emotional space–and what stays out. This is the Principle of Emotional Filtering.

Emotional Filtering means:

Recognize emotional overload:

When you feel drained, ask: "Is this mine?" Often, you're carrying emotions that belong to someone else.

Set clear boundaries with kindness:

You can say "I need space," or "I can't talk about this right now," without being harsh. Boundaries are not rejection–they're protection.

Use grounding techniques:

When emotions feel overwhelming, breathe deeply. Visualize a boundary around you. Remind yourself: "I am allowed to protect my peace."

Practice emotional detachment:

Care without carrying. Listen without absorbing. Support without sacrificing your own well-being.

Reaffirm your limits regularly:

Boundaries need maintenance. Check in with yourself often: "What do I need to feel safe and balanced?"

This principle is a turning point. When you build emotional boundaries, you stop being a sponge–and start being a person with clarity, strength, and self-respect. You rise–not by shutting people out, but by keeping yourself whole.

Chapter 7
Choosing Peace Over Perfection

"I've realized that being happy is a choice. You never want to look back and think, why was I so unhappy when I had so much?"

Angelina Jolie

Perfection promises control, approval, and success. But what it often delivers is stress, self-doubt, and burnout. The pursuit of perfection can feel noble–like you're striving to be your best. But when it becomes a constant pressure, it robs you of peace. You start measuring your worth by flawless outcomes, and anything less feels like failure.

Choosing peace over perfection is a radical shift. It means valuing your well-being more than your performance. It means accepting that mistakes, messiness, and imperfection are part of being human. And it's one of the most liberating steps in rising from negativity, stress, and loneliness.

How It Feels

Choosing peace over perfection feels like:

Letting go of the need to impress, and choosing to be authentic.

Feeling relief when you allow yourself to rest instead of overwork.

Accepting that "good enough" is often more than enough.

Releasing the fear of judgment and embracing self-compassion.

Feeling lighter, freer, and more connected to yourself.

At first, it feels unfamiliar—even wrong. But over time, it feels like coming home to yourself.

Real-Life Examples

In Academics or Work:

Meera spends hours perfecting every assignment, every email, every presentation. She's praised for her excellence—but she's exhausted. One day, she submits a project without obsessing over every detail. It's still good. She feels calm. She realizes peace matters more than praise.

In Parenting:

Ravi wants to be the perfect father. He plans every activity, worries about every decision. But his child just wants his presence. When Ravi lets go of the pressure and simply plays, listens, and laughs—he feels more connected. His child feels more loved.

In Social Media:

Aarushi edits every photo, every caption, trying to present a flawless life. But it feels fake. One day, she posts something real—unedited, honest. The response is warm. She feels seen. Peace replaces performance.

In Healing:

Karan wants to "fix" himself quickly. He reads, meditates, journals—but still feels broken. Eventually, he stops trying to be perfect and starts being present. He allows himself to heal slowly, imperfectly. That's when real growth begins.

A Principle to Rise: The Principle of Gentle Acceptance

Perfection is rigid. Peace is flexible. The way to rise is to stop chasing flawless and start embracing real. This is the Principle of Gentle Acceptance.

Gentle Acceptance means:

Redefine success:

Ask yourself: "Does this need to be perfect–or just honest?" Often, authenticity matters more than precision.

Practice self-compassion:

When you make a mistake, speak kindly to yourself. Say, "It's okay. I'm learning." Perfection punishes–peace forgives.

Set realistic expectations:

You don't have to do everything. You don't have to do it all perfectly. Choose what matters–and let the rest go.

Celebrate effort, not just outcome:

Acknowledge your progress, your courage, your consistency. These are victories too.

Create space for rest and joy:

Perfection demands constant effort. Peace invites balance. Make time for things that nourish you–not just things that prove you.

This principle is a turning point. When you choose peace over perfection, you stop performing and start living. You rise–not because you're flawless, but because you're free.

Chapter 8
Trusting Yourself Again

"As soon as you trust yourself, you will know how to live."

Johan Wolfgang von Goethe

There's a quiet kind of pain that comes from doubting your own voice. You second-guess your choices, question your feelings, and hesitate to act. You look to others for answers, afraid that yours might be wrong. This loss of self-trust doesn't happen overnight–it builds slowly, often after repeated disappointments, criticism, or emotional wounds.

But here's the truth: you were born with intuition. With wisdom. With a voice that knows what you need. Trusting yourself again isn't about being perfect–it's about reconnecting with that voice. It's about believing that your feelings are valid, your choices are worthy, and your path is yours to walk.

This shift is essential in rising from stress, negativity, and loneliness. Because when you trust yourself, you stop abandoning yourself–and start coming home.

How It Feels

Trusting yourself again feels like:

Listening to your gut, even when others disagree.

Making decisions without needing constant reassurance.

Feeling confident in your boundaries, your needs, your truth.

Accepting that mistakes are part of growth—not proof of failure.

Feeling grounded, even in uncertainty.

At first, it feels shaky. You'll still doubt. You'll still seek validation. But with time, it becomes strength. You begin to feel whole again.

Real-Life Examples

After a Toxic Relationship:

Meera was in a relationship where her feelings were constantly dismissed. She started believing she was "too emotional" or "always wrong." After the breakup, she struggles to trust her instincts. But slowly, she starts journaling, reflecting, and making small decisions on her own. Each time she listens to herself, her confidence grows.

In Career Choices:

Ravi left a stable job to pursue something more meaningful. People questioned him. He doubted himself. But he kept going. He reminded himself why he made the choice. Eventually, his new path brings fulfillment—and he learns that trusting himself was the right move.

In Everyday Decisions:

Aarushi often asks friends for advice—even on small things. She fears making the wrong choice. But she starts practicing self-trust: choosing her outfit, planning her day, making decisions without polling others. She feels more empowered, more independent.

In Emotional Healing:

Karan has been told for years to "toughen up." He learned to suppress his emotions. But now, he's learning to trust his feelings. When he feels sad, he allows it. When he feels joy, he embraces it. His emotions become guides–not enemies.

A Principle to Rise: The Principle of Inner Trust

You are your own compass. The way to rise is to stop outsourcing your truth and start believing in your own wisdom. This is the Principle of Inner Trust.

Inner Trust means:

Listen before you ask:

Before seeking advice, ask yourself: "What do I feel? What do I want?" Your voice matters.

Validate your emotions:

Every feeling has a reason. You don't need permission to feel. Say to yourself: "It's okay to feel this."

Make small decisions independently:

Start with everyday choices. Build confidence through action. Trust grows with practice.

Reflect on past wins:

Remember times you trusted yourself–and it worked out. Let those memories remind you of your strength.

Forgive your mistakes:

Self-trust doesn't mean being right all the time. It means knowing you'll learn, adapt, and grow–no matter what.

This principle is a turning point. When you trust yourself again, you stop living in fear and start living in alignment. You rise–not because others believe in you, but because you believe in yourself.

Chapter 9
Making Space for Joy

"Joy does not simply happen to us. We have to choose joy and keep choosing it every day."

Henri Nouwen

When life feels heavy, joy can seem distant–like a luxury you can't afford. You're busy surviving, managing stress, navigating loneliness. Joy feels out of place, even suspicious. You wonder, "How can I feel happy when so much is wrong?" But joy isn't a reward for having a perfect life. It's a necessity for healing. It's a light that reminds you there's still beauty, even in the middle of pain.

Making space for joy doesn't mean ignoring your struggles. It means allowing joy to coexist with them. It's a shift from waiting for happiness to arrive, to inviting it in–right here, right now.

How It Feels

Making space for joy feels like:

Laughing without guilt, even when things aren't perfect.

Noticing small moments–sunlight through a window, a kind message, a favorite song.

Feeling warmth in your chest, even if your heart is still healing.

Allowing yourself to enjoy something without overthinking it.

Realizing that joy doesn't erase pain—it balances it.

At first, joy feels unfamiliar. You might resist it, question it, or feel undeserving. But with time, it becomes a companion. A reminder that you're still alive. Still capable of feeling. Still worthy of light.

Real-Life Examples

In Daily Life:

Meera is going through a tough breakup. She feels numb most days. But one morning, she hears her favorite song and starts dancing in her room. For those few minutes, she feels alive. That joy doesn't fix everything—but it gives her strength to keep going.

In Parenting:

Ravi is overwhelmed with responsibilities. He's tired, stressed, and constantly worried. But one evening, his child tells a silly joke, and they both burst into laughter. That moment of joy becomes a memory he holds onto during harder days.

In Solitude:

Aarushi lives alone and often feels lonely. But she starts a small ritual—making tea and watching the sunset. It becomes her daily joy. A moment of peace that reminds her she can create beauty, even in solitude.

In Healing:

Karan is recovering from anxiety. He journals, meditates, and works on himself. But he also starts painting again—something he loved as a child. That creative joy becomes part of his healing, not separate from it.

A Principle to Rise: The Principle of Joyful Permission

Joy doesn't need a perfect setting–it needs permission. The way to rise is to stop postponing joy and start welcoming it into your life. This is the Principle of Joyful Permission.

Joyful Permission means:

Let joy in, even when life is messy:

You don't have to wait for everything to be okay. Joy is allowed, even in the middle of healing.

Notice the small things:

Joy often hides in ordinary moments. A smile, a breeze, a memory. Pay attention. Let them matter.

Create joy intentionally:

Schedule time for things that make you happy–music, art, nature, connection. Joy needs space to grow.

Release guilt around happiness:

Feeling joy doesn't mean you're ignoring your pain. It means you're choosing balance. Say to yourself: "I'm allowed to feel good."

Share joy with others:

Joy multiplies when shared. Send a kind message. Share a laugh. Celebrate small wins. Connection deepens joy.

This principle is a turning point. When you make space for joy, you stop waiting for life to be perfect–and start living it as it is. You rise–not by escaping your pain, but by letting joy walk beside it.

Chapter 10
The Power of Small Wins

"Look for small victories and build on that. Each small victory, even if it is just getting up five minutes earlier, gives you confidence.

Arnold Schwarzenegger

When life feels overwhelming, progress can seem impossible. You look at the distance between where you are and where you want to be–and it feels too far. So you freeze. You wait for a breakthrough, a big change, a dramatic shift. But healing doesn't happen in leaps. It happens in steps. And those steps are often small, quiet, and easily overlooked.

Small wins are the building blocks of transformation. They're the moments when you choose to get out of bed, speak kindly to yourself, take a deep breath instead of reacting, or finish something you've been avoiding. They may not look impressive–but they matter. Because every small win is proof that you're moving forward.

How It Feels

The power of small wins feels like:

A quiet sense of pride after completing something you've been putting off.

Feeling more capable, even if the task was simple.

Noticing that your mindset is slowly shifting.

Realizing that progress doesn't have to be loud to be real.

Feeling encouraged to keep going, one step at a time.

At first, small wins feel insignificant. You might dismiss them. But when you start noticing and celebrating them, they become fuel. They remind you that you're not stuck—you're growing.

Real-Life Examples

In Mental Health:

Meera struggles with anxiety. Some days, even getting out of bed feels hard. But she starts tracking small wins: brushing her teeth, going for a walk, replying to one message. Each win builds momentum. She begins to feel more in control—not because the anxiety is gone, but because she's showing up anyway.

In Work and Productivity:

Ravi feels overwhelmed by his to-do list. He used to wait until he had the energy to tackle everything. Now, he focuses on one task at a time. Sending one email. Organizing one folder. Each small win reduces stress and builds confidence.

In Emotional Healing:

Aarushi is grieving a loss. She doesn't feel ready to "move on." But she starts noticing small wins: smiling at a memory, cooking a meal, talking to a friend. These moments don't erase the pain—but they show her that healing is happening.

In Building Habits:

Karan wants to start journaling but keeps procrastinating. Instead of aiming for a full page, he writes one sentence a day. That small win becomes a habit. Over time, it grows into a powerful tool for self-reflection.

A Principle to Rise: The Principle of Micro-Momentum

Big change begins with small movement. The way to rise is to stop waiting for perfect conditions and start building momentum through tiny victories. This is the Principle of Micro-Momentum.

Micro-Momentum means:

Break goals into small actions:

Instead of "fix everything," try "do one thing." Progress becomes possible when it's manageable.

Track your wins daily:

Write down three small things you did today. Celebrate them. Let them remind you that you're moving.

Shift your focus from outcome to effort:

Don't wait for big results to feel proud. Honor the effort. Showing up is a win.

Use small wins to build confidence:

Each win proves you're capable. Let that proof fuel your next step.

Be consistent, not perfect:

Small wins repeated over time create lasting change. Consistency matters more than intensity.

This principle is a turning point. When you start honoring your small wins, you stop feeling stuck and start feeling strong. You rise—not in one giant leap, but in a thousand quiet steps.

Part Five

Rising, Slowly

Chapter 1
Healing Isn't Linear

"I've been through a lot of mental, physical, and emotional pain. But I'm still here. Healing is ongoing."

Lady Gaga

"Healing is not a one-time event. It's a daily decision to choose yourself."

Glennon Doyle

Healing is not a straight road. It doesn't follow a neat timeline or offer predictable milestones. It's more like a winding path through a forest—sometimes clear, sometimes foggy, sometimes uphill. You may feel strong one day and fragile the next. You may think you've moved past something, only to find it resurfacing in a quiet moment. And that doesn't mean you're failing. It means you're healing.

We often expect progress to look like constant improvement. But real healing is full of pauses, setbacks, and unexpected emotions. It's crying after weeks of calm. It's feeling triggered by something you thought you'd outgrown. It's needing rest when you thought you were ready to run. And all of it is valid.

Take Meera, for example. After leaving a toxic relationship, she felt empowered. She started therapy, made new friends, and began rebuilding her life. But one evening, while watching a movie, a scene reminded her of her past. She broke down. For a moment, she felt like she was back at the beginning. But her therapist reminded her: "This isn't regression. It's a wave. And you're learning to ride it." That moment didn't erase her progress–it deepened it. It reminded her that healing isn't about never hurting again. It's about knowing how to hold yourself when you do.

Healing asks for patience. It asks you to be gentle with yourself when things feel hard again. It asks you to trust that even when you feel like you're standing still, something inside you is shifting. You're learning. You're growing. You're rising–slowly, but surely.

There will be days when you feel like you're moving backward. Let them pass. There will be days when you feel strong again. Let them stay. The journey isn't perfect, but it's yours. And every step, even the shaky ones, are part of your becoming.

Chapter 2
You're Allowed to Rest

"Rest is the best medicine."

Barbara Ann Kipfer

"Don't sacrifice yourself too much, because if you sacrifice too much there's nothing else you can give and nobody will care for you."

Karl Lagerfeld

In a world that glorifies hustle, rest can feel like weakness. We're taught to keep going, keep producing, keep proving. But healing asks for something different. It asks for stillness. It asks for softness. It asks for rest—not as a reward, but as a requirement.

You're allowed to rest. Not just when you've earned it, but when you need it. Rest is not quitting. It's not giving up. It's a way of honoring your limits, listening to your body, and respecting your emotional capacity. It's how you recharge, how you reconnect, how you rise—slowly, but steadily.

Rest doesn't always look like sleep. Sometimes it's stepping away from a draining conversation. Sometimes it's saying no to one more task.

Sometimes it's sitting in silence, letting your thoughts settle. And sometimes, it's doing absolutely nothing—and letting that be enough.

Take Aarushi, for example. She's been juggling work, family, and her own emotional healing. She's been pushing herself to stay strong, to stay productive. But one morning, she wakes up feeling heavy. Instead of forcing herself through the day, she chooses to rest. She cancels a meeting, takes a walk, and spends the afternoon reading. That simple act of rest doesn't fix everything—but it shifts something inside her. She feels calmer. More present. More herself.

Rest is not a pause in your progress—it's part of it. It's the space where your mind clears, your heart softens, and your strength returns. When you allow yourself to rest, you send a powerful message to yourself: "I matter. My well-being matters." And that message is healing in itself.

You don't have to earn rest. You don't have to justify it. You just have to allow it. Because rising from stress, negativity, and loneliness isn't about constant motion—it's about learning when to stop, breathe, and simply be.

Chapter 3
Confidence Without Ego

"We come nearest to the great when we are great in humility."

Rabindranath Tagore

Confidence is not about being the loudest voice in the room or the most dominant presence–it's about knowing your worth without needing to announce it. It's the quiet assurance that comes from doing the work, failing forward, and learning deeply. Ego, on the other hand, is a fragile mask that demands attention and validation. It thrives on comparison and competition, while confidence is rooted in self-awareness and growth. When you're truly confident, you don't need to prove anything. You listen more than you speak, you ask questions without fear of looking uninformed, and you celebrate others without feeling diminished.

The most powerful people are often the most humble. They walk into a room and don't need to posture because their presence speaks for itself. Confidence without ego means you can admit when you're wrong, take feedback without defensiveness, and detach your self-worth from outcomes. It's not about being perfect–it's about being real. You don't shrink to be humble, and you don't inflate to be strong. You stand firm in your values, knowing that your identity isn't tied to external validation.

To build this kind of confidence, you must practice radical self-honesty. Know your strengths and own your weaknesses. Master something deeply—not to impress others, but to trust yourself. Ask more questions than you answer, because curiosity is a sign of strength, not ignorance. Celebrate others publicly, because ego competes while confidence collaborates. And most importantly, detach from results. Ego ties your worth to success; confidence ties it to effort and integrity.

Take Priya, a young woman working in a fast-paced marketing firm. She's not the loudest in meetings, nor does she constantly push her ideas to the front. But when she speaks, people listen—because she's thoughtful, prepared, and grounded. One day, her team was struggling with a campaign that wasn't landing well. Instead of jumping in to take credit or dominate the conversation, Priya asked smart questions, encouraged quieter teammates to share their thoughts, and calmly suggested a new angle based on data she'd quietly gathered over the past week.

Her manager later praised her—not just for the idea, but for how she led with humility and clarity. Priya didn't need to boast or compete. Her confidence came from knowing her work, trusting her instincts, and respecting others. That's confidence without ego: showing up fully, without needing to overshadow anyone else. It's the kind of energy that builds trust, earns respect, and creates space for everyone to thrive.

Chapter 4
Self-Esteem from the Inside Out

"I have insecurities of course, but I don't hang out with anyone who points them out to me."

Adele

Self-esteem isn't something you're born with–it's something you build, moment by moment, choice by choice. It's not loud or showy, and it doesn't need to be announced. Real self-esteem is quiet, steady, and deeply personal. It's the feeling that you are enough–not because of what you've achieved or how others see you, but because you've come to know and accept yourself. It's not about being flawless; it's about being honest. When you live in alignment with your values, when you treat yourself with respect, and when you show up even when it's hard, you begin to trust yourself. That trust is the foundation of self-esteem.

Most people chase self-worth through external validation. They seek praise, attention, and approval, hoping it will fill the void inside. But that kind of esteem is fragile. It rises and falls with other people's opinions. True self-esteem comes from within. It's built when you keep promises to yourself, when you speak kindly to yourself, and when you forgive yourself for being human. It's not about being liked–it's about being real. You stop performing and start living. You stop chasing and start creating. You stop hiding and start showing up.

The way you talk to yourself matters more than anything else. If your inner voice is harsh, critical, or dismissive, no amount of compliments will make you feel whole. But when your inner voice is compassionate, firm, and encouraging, you begin to feel safe with yourself. You stop needing to prove your worth, because you already know it. You start making choices that reflect your values, not your fears. You begin to live from a place of integrity, not insecurity. That's the shift—from outside-in to inside-out.

Aarushi used to feel good about herself mostly when people complimented her—on her looks, her work, or her personality. If someone praised her, she'd feel confident for a while, but the moment that praise stopped or someone criticized her, her mood would crash. She didn't realize how much her self-worth depended on others until she started making small changes. Instead of waiting for compliments, she began spending more time doing things that made her feel proud—like helping her younger cousin with schoolwork, finishing tasks she'd been putting off, and speaking up when something bothered her. She also started paying attention to how she felt after certain conversations or decisions, noticing when she felt strong and when she felt drained. Slowly, she began to feel good about herself not because someone said she was amazing, but because she knew she was showing up with honesty, kindness, and courage. Her confidence stopped depending on being seen—it started growing from how she saw herself.

Rohan had always been the dependable boyfriend—the one who showed up, remembered the little things, and tried to be everything his partner needed. But somewhere along the way, he started losing sight of himself. If his girlfriend was upset, he'd immediately assume he was the problem. If she needed space, he'd feel rejected. His self-esteem became tied to how well he could keep her happy. Slowly, he stopped doing things he enjoyed, stopped expressing his own needs, and started shrinking himself to fit into what he thought a "good boyfriend" should be.

One evening, after a quiet dinner where he felt invisible, Rohan realized he had abandoned his own emotional center. He wasn't showing up for himself—only for someone else. So he decided to make a shift. He began reconnecting with the things that made him feel alive: playing guitar, going for solo runs, spending time with friends without guilt. He started journaling—not about the relationship, but about his own thoughts, feelings, and goals. He practiced speaking up gently when something bothered him, even if it felt uncomfortable. He stopped interpreting silence as rejection and began trusting his own emotional resilience.

As Rohan grew more grounded in himself, the relationship began to feel healthier. He was no longer seeking constant reassurance, and his girlfriend noticed the change. He became more confident, more relaxed, and more emotionally present—not because she changed, but because he did. His self-esteem was no longer dependent on being the perfect partner. It was rooted in self-respect, in knowing that he mattered even when things weren't perfect. That's self-esteem from the inside out: choosing to be whole, not just helpful.

Chapter 5
Reconnecting with Hope

"I don't think of all the misery, but of the beauty that still remains."

Anne Frank, diarist and Holocaust victim

Hope isn't about ignoring pain or pretending everything is fine–it's about believing that things can get better, even when they've been really hard. It's not loud or dramatic. Sometimes, it's just a quiet thought that says, "Maybe tomorrow won't be as heavy as today." Reconnecting with hope doesn't mean you forget what hurt you. It means you stop letting that pain decide everything. It's the moment you choose to look forward, even if you're still healing. Hope doesn't fix everything overnight, but it gives you the strength to keep going. It's like a small light that helps you take one more step, even when the path isn't clear.

Meera had been through a rough few years. She lost a job she loved, went through a breakup that left her feeling empty, and started doubting herself in ways she never had before. She stopped making plans, stopped dreaming, and even stopped doing the little things that used to bring her joy–like painting or going for evening walks. Every day felt like just getting through. But one morning, while scrolling through old photos, she saw a picture of herself smiling at a beach, holding a sketchbook. Something about that moment reminded her of who she used to be–not perfect, but hopeful. That day, she didn't make a big change. She just stepped outside, sat in the sun for a few minutes, and let herself imagine what life could feel like if she started caring again.

Over the next few weeks, Meera didn't force herself to be happy. She just started doing small things—calling a friend, cooking her favorite meal, applying for one job even though she was scared of rejection. Slowly, she began to feel a shift. Not because everything was fixed, but because she was moving again. She had something to walk toward. That's what hope looks like in real life. It's not dramatic or perfect. It's choosing to believe in better days, even when you've seen the worst. It's giving yourself permission to try again.

Chapter 6
Loving Yourself in Pieces

"Treat yourself like you'd treat your best friend ... Be your own best friend."

Jameela Jamil, actress and activist

You don't have to wait until everything in your life feels perfect to start loving yourself. You don't need to be completely healed, confident, or sorted out. Real self-love begins when you stop waiting to feel "ready" and start accepting yourself as you are–flaws, fears, and all. It's not about ignoring the messy parts; it's about choosing to be kind to them. Loving yourself in pieces means looking at the parts you usually hide or criticize and saying, "This part matters too." It's choosing compassion over judgment, even when you feel broken or unsure.

Karan had been feeling overwhelmed lately. His income wasn't growing the way he hoped, and every time he thought about the future, he felt a wave of anxiety. He worried that one day everyone he loved would be gone–that people would die, and he'd be left alone. That thought made him sad, even on days when nothing was actually wrong. He was also stressed about being older and still unmarried, and deep down, he feared that his girlfriend might leave him someday. These thoughts didn't just come and go–they stayed, quietly draining his energy and making it hard to feel cheerful, even when good things happened.

But instead of pushing those feelings away or pretending they didn't exist, Karan began to face them gently. He didn't try to fix everything at once. He started by talking to a close friend, someone who didn't judge him and just listened. He began taking small steps to care for himself–like going for walks, spending time with people who made him feel safe, and reminding himself that it was okay to feel this way. He didn't wait to feel perfect before showing himself kindness. He chose to love himself in the middle of the mess. Slowly, he began to feel more grounded–not because the fears disappeared, but because he stopped running from them. That's what loving yourself in pieces looks like: accepting your fears, your sadness, and your imperfections, and still choosing to treat yourself with care.

Chapter 7
Resilience: Showing Up Anyway

"I have not failed. I've just found 10,000 ways that won't work."

Thomas Edison, inventor

Resilience isn't about being strong all the time–it's about showing up even when you feel broken, tired, or unsure. Some days, you won't feel ready. You'll wake up with a heavy chest, a mind full of worries, and no motivation to face the day. But resilience is built in those exact moments–when you choose to keep going, not because you feel powerful, but because you refuse to give up. According to the American Psychological Association, resilience is the ability to adapt and recover from adversity. It's not something you're born with–it's something you build through small, consistent choices.

Aarushi had recently lost her mother, and nothing felt normal anymore. Her mother had been her emotional anchor–the one person who understood her without words. After the funeral, life kept moving, but Aarushi didn't. She stopped cooking, avoided calls, and barely slept. Even getting out of bed felt like a task. She didn't feel ready to return to work or talk to friends. But one morning, she decided to do just one thing: wash her face and step outside for a few minutes. That small act didn't fix her grief, but it helped her breathe.

Over the next few weeks, Aarushi didn't try to "bounce back." She focused on doing what she could. She started replying to one or two messages a day, even if it was just a short "thank you." She asked her manager for flexible hours and took on lighter tasks. She didn't force herself to socialize, but she did say yes when a close friend invited her for chai. She kept her meals simple—sometimes just toast and tea—but she ate. She didn't pretend to be okay, but she showed up in small ways: brushing her hair, folding laundry, sitting through a meeting even when her mind wandered.

These weren't big, dramatic steps. They were quiet, ordinary choices that helped her feel a little more stable. Aarushi still missed her mother deeply. Some days, the sadness hit her out of nowhere. But she learned that resilience isn't about pushing through—it's about gently continuing. It's about showing up in your grief, in your messiness, and in your fear. And every time she did, she reminded herself: "I'm still here. I'm still trying." That's resilience—not perfection, but presence.

Chapter 8
Becoming Your Own Safe Place

"You can't really be present for other people if you're not present for yourself."

Kerry Washington, actress

Feeling safe isn't just about your surroundings–it's about how you treat yourself when life feels unstable. Becoming your own safe place means learning to calm your thoughts, protect your peace, and make choices that help you feel secure both emotionally and practically. It's about knowing that even when someone hurts you, leaves you, or misunderstands you, you can still return to yourself. And there's no age limit to start this journey. Whether you're 22 or 52, you can begin building a life where you feel supported from the inside out.

Ravi used to fall apart after conflict. If someone fought with him–especially someone close–he'd feel anxious, rejected, and desperate to feel okay again. He'd immediately reach out to others, hoping someone would comfort him or distract him. But over time, he realized that relying on others to feel safe wasn't sustainable. He wanted to feel steady even when things around him weren't.

So he began trying small, practical steps to soothe himself after conflict. One of the first things he did was go for brisk walks with a timer–20 minutes, no phone, just movement. He found that walking helped release tension and gave him space to think clearly. He also started telling himself, "This will pass. It always does," reminding himself of past situations that felt overwhelming but eventually faded. Sometimes, he'd go shopping—not to spend impulsively, but to buy something small that made him feel cared for, like a fresh shirt or his favorite snack. Other times, he'd clean his room or organize a drawer—simple tasks that gave him a sense of control when everything else felt chaotic.

He also began setting boundaries with himself. If he felt the urge to text someone out of panic, he'd wait 10 minutes and ask, "Do I need comfort, or do I need clarity?" That pause helped him respond instead of react. He started keeping his evenings gentle—watching a familiar movie, cooking something easy, or just sitting quietly with a cup of tea. And most importantly, he began managing his finances. He created a basic budget, started saving a little each month, and made sure he had enough for unexpected situations. That financial stability gave him a sense of safety that no relationship could replace.

Ravi didn't become emotionally bulletproof. He still felt sad, still had bad days. But he stopped outsourcing his peace. He learned that being your own safe place doesn't mean you don't need people—it means you don't collapse when they're not there. It means you know how to take care of yourself when things get hard. And that kind of safety—emotional and financial—is something you can start building today, no matter where you are in life.

Chapter 9
Your Story Isn't Over

"If you are still breathing, you have a second chance."

Oprah Winfrey, media mogul and philanthropist

No matter what you've been through, your story isn't over. Life doesn't stop at heartbreak, failure, or loss–it keeps moving, and so do you. You may carry pain, regrets, or scars, but none of them define your future. Every day is a fresh page. Every decision is a new sentence. And you are still the author. This truth is powerful because it reminds you that you're not stuck–you're evolving. Healing isn't about erasing the past; it's about choosing what comes next, even when the past still hurts.

There are people who've faced unimaginable setbacks and still found a way forward. Sudha Chandran, a renowned Indian dancer and actress, lost her leg in a road accident. Most would have given up–but she didn't. She learned to dance with a prosthetic leg and went on to inspire millions with her performances and strength. Her story is a reminder that physical loss doesn't mean the end of your passion.

Nick Vujicic, born without arms or legs, struggled deeply with depression and bullying. But instead of letting his condition define him, he chose to rise. Today, he's a global motivational speaker, author, and founder of Life Without Limbs. His life proves that limitations don't have to limit your impact.

These stories aren't just headlines—they're proof that life doesn't end at your lowest point. You can lose everything and still rebuild. You can be broken and still rise. You can feel stuck and still move forward. Whether you're dealing with grief, financial stress, heartbreak, or just feeling lost, your story isn't finished. You don't need a perfect plan. You just need to take one step, and then another. You're allowed to start over. You're allowed to change. And you're allowed to believe that something good can still come from where you are now.

Chapter 10
Letting Go of Guilt: You're Allowed to Move Forward

"As long as you don't forgive, who and whatever it is will occupy a rent-free space in your mind."

Isabelle Holland, novelist

Guilt is one of the heaviest emotions we carry. It doesn't always come from doing something wrong–it often comes from what we didn't do. Words we didn't say. Goodbyes we missed. Decisions we made without knowing their full impact. And while guilt can teach us, it can also trap us. Letting go of guilt isn't about pretending it didn't happen–it's about accepting that we're human, learning from it, and choosing to move forward with more care. Guilt, while heavy, isn't meant to be permanent. It's meant to teach, then release. You're allowed to feel it–but you're also allowed to move forward.

The Son Who Missed His Father's Goodbye

Raghav had moved abroad for his studies, excited about the future. In the rush of packing and planning, he gave his father a quick hug and left, thinking there'd be time later. But months into his course, he got the call–his father had passed away suddenly. No final words. No proper goodbye. The guilt was crushing. He felt like he'd failed as a son.

How he coped:

- He allowed himself to grieve fully, without rushing to "be okay."
- He began calling his mother regularly, building a deeper connection.
- He visited his father's favorite places when he returned home, not to mourn, but to feel close.
- He started showing up more intentionally in relationships—never leaving things unsaid.
- He forgave himself by remembering that love isn't measured by one moment, but by a lifetime of care.

The Man Who Gave a Poor Rating

Aman had taken his Mercedes to a service center. The car stayed longer than expected, and out of frustration, he gave a poor rating online. Later, he learned that the rating had impacted the salary of the advisor—the only person who had treated him kindly. The guilt was sharp.

How he coped:

- He returned to the center and apologized directly to the advisor.
- He submitted a revised review and wrote to the management to explain.
- He promised himself to pause before reacting next time.
- He began tipping generously and expressing appreciation more consciously.

The Grandchild Who Never Said "I Love You"

Nandini adored her grandmother but never said "I love you" out loud. After her grandmother passed, that unsaid phrase became a source of pain.

How she coped:

- She began talking about her grandmother often, keeping her memory alive.
- She started expressing love more openly to others.
- She created small rituals–lighting a candle, playing her grandmother's favorite song.
- She forgave herself by remembering that love is felt, even when unspoken.

The Man Who Didn't Pursue His Dream Job

Sameer had always wanted to be a wildlife photographer. But he chose a corporate job instead–safe, stable, and expected. Years passed, and the dream faded. Now in his 40s, he felt a deep guilt for not trying. He wondered what life could've been if he'd taken the risk.

How he coped:

- He didn't quit everything overnight. He started small–weekend trips to nearby forests, clicking photos just for joy.
- He joined an online community of hobby photographers, sharing his work and learning from others.
- He began volunteering with a local conservation group, reconnecting with his passion.

- He stopped seeing his past as wasted and started seeing it as experience that could support his dream now.
- He reminded himself: it's never too late to begin again.

Letting go of guilt is not a single moment—it's a gradual process that unfolds through small, intentional choices. It begins with acknowledging the regret honestly, without trying to bury or deny it. Then comes the step of making amends, if possible—whether through a sincere apology, a corrective action, or simply showing up differently moving forward. Learning from the experience is key, not to punish yourself, but to grow with more awareness. Practicing self-forgiveness is often the hardest part, but it's essential; it means reminding yourself that being human includes making mistakes. And finally, letting go means choosing to live with intention, not shame—allowing your past to inform you, but not imprison you. Guilt may be part of your story, but it doesn't have to be the ending.

Part Six

Rising with Freedom

Chapter 1
Spending to Feel Seen

"We buy things we don't need with money
we don't have to impress people we don't like."

Dave Ramsey, financial expert and author

Sometimes, we don't buy things because we need them–we buy them because we need to feel something. A sense of worth. A moment of control. A glimpse of recognition. In a world that constantly tells us who we should be, what we should wear, and how we should present ourselves, spending can become a way to say, "I matter." It's not just about the product–it's about the feeling behind the purchase.

For many, shopping becomes emotional. You're not just buying a new outfit–you're buying confidence for the party you're nervous about. You're not just upgrading your phone–you're trying to keep up with friends who seem ahead. You're not just booking a luxury stay–you're trying to feel like you belong in a life that looks better than yours on social media. These moments aren't shallow–they're human. But when spending becomes the only way we feel seen, it starts to cost more than money.

Celebrities have spoken openly about this. Tyra Banks admitted she used to shop to feel better about herself, only to realize no handbag could fix what was going on inside. Jay-Z reflected on how he once tied his value to brands and cars, until he learned that real success is peace of mind. Even Demi Lovato shared how she spent money trying to look like she had it all together, while feeling broken inside.

The truth is, visibility doesn't come from what you own—it comes from how you see yourself. When you begin to validate your own worth, you stop needing purchases to do it for you. That doesn't mean you stop shopping—it means you start choosing with clarity, not desperation. You buy the shoes because you love them, not because you think they'll make someone love you.

Real-Life Examples

- *Neha*, 28, worked in digital marketing and often felt invisible in her relationship. After arguments with her partner, she'd scroll through shopping apps late at night, buying clothes she didn't need. The packages gave her a fleeting sense of control and beauty—like she was curating a version of herself that deserved attention. But the thrill faded quickly, replaced by guilt and unopened boxes. It wasn't until she began journaling her emotions before purchases that she realized she was trying to buy the love she wasn't receiving.
- *Arjun*, 35, grew up in a lower-middle-class household where money was tight and status mattered. Now a successful architect, he felt compelled to pick up the tab at dinners, even when it strained him. He feared being seen as "cheap" or "still poor." One day, a close friend gently asked, "Why do you always pay?" That question cracked something open. Arjun began exploring his relationship with money and worth, eventually learning to share expenses without shame.

A Principle to Rise: The Principle of Emotional Spending Awareness

Spending isn't just financial–it's emotional. The way to rise is to notice the feeling behind the purchase. This is the Principle of Emotional Spending Awareness.

Emotional Spending Awareness means:

- Name the emotion before you buy–loneliness, shame, boredom?
- Use the "Pause and Purpose" test: Is this for comfort or function?
- Keep a "Want vs. Need" journal to track patterns.
- Replace spending rituals with self-care rituals.
- Celebrate restraint as a form of self-respect.

Chapter 2
Budgeting with Compassion

"Money is only a tool. It will take you wherever you wish, but it will not replace you as the driver."

Ayn Rand

Budgeting isn't just about numbers–it's about care. It's about making choices that support your life, your values, and your peace of mind. Too often, people think of budgeting as something strict or punishing. But when done with compassion, budgeting becomes a way to take care of yourself–not control yourself.

Compassionate budgeting means understanding your habits without judgment. It means asking, *Why did I spend that?* instead of *What's wrong with me?* It's about creating space for joy, not just cutting costs. You're not trying to be perfect–you're trying to be honest. And that honesty helps you build a life that feels safe, balanced, and aligned with what matters most.

Instead of asking, "*Where did all my money go?*" at the end of the month, try this: Create a simple Excel sheet for your monthly budget. Just list your income, your fixed expenses (like rent, bills, groceries), and your flexible spending (like eating out, shopping, entertainment). Every time you spend, make a quick entry. At the end of the month, you'll see clearly where your money went–and how much you saved. If making a sheet from scratch feels overwhelming, don't worry. There are plenty of free monthly budget templates available online that you can download and customize. It's not about perfection. It's about awareness.

Real-Life Examples

- *Meenal*, 26, had grown up in a household where budgeting was a punishment—something done only when things were falling apart. As an adult, she avoided it entirely. But after a panic attack triggered by a surprise bill, she decided to try again. This time, she created a colorful spreadsheet with categories like "Joy," "Healing," and "Adventure." She added stickers, quotes, and even a playlist. Budgeting became a ritual of self-care, not self-criticism.
- *Kabir*, 38, had accumulated debt after a failed startup. Every time he opened his banking app, he felt nauseous. He started calling his budget a "freedom map" and tracked emotional wins—like choosing home-cooked meals over takeout or saying no to impulse buys. Slowly, his anxiety softened, and his confidence returned.

A Principle to Rise: The Principle of Gentle Structure

Budgets should feel like support, not punishment. The way to rise is to build a structure that reflects your values. This is the Principle of Gentle Structure.

Gentle Structure means:

- Ask yourself what feels good, not just what looks good. Does this budget reflect who I am and what I care about?
- Track progress, not perfection. Some months will be messy. That's okay. Look for patterns, not punishments.

- Revisit your budget with kindness. Set aside time once a month to reflect not to criticize, but to adjust gently.
- Keep your goals visible. Whether it's a vacation, a debt-free life, or just peace of mind–remind yourself why you're doing this.
- Stay consistent, even when it's not exciting. The first month might feel empowering. The second might even be fun. But by the third, it can feel repetitive. That's normal. Budgeting is like brushing your teeth–it's not thrilling, but it keeps things healthy. The real results come from showing up month after month, even when motivation fades.

Chapter 3
Earning Without Shame

If you're investing your time and effort into meaningful work, it deserves fair compensation.

Yogesh Dhiman

There's a quiet guilt that follows many people when they start earning from something they love—or something that helps others. Artists, therapists, teachers, caregivers, even those who write or coach—often feel a tug of discomfort when money enters the picture. The world has long whispered that "helping shouldn't be profitable," or that creativity is only pure if it's unpaid. But that narrative is not only outdated—it's harmful.

Earning is not exploitation. It's sustainability.

You're not greedy for wanting to be paid. You're responsible. You're building a life where your work can continue, where your energy isn't drained, and where your gifts aren't buried under burnout. When you earn with integrity, you're not taking—you're creating space to keep giving.

Think about it: a therapist who charges for sessions isn't selfish. They're making it possible to show up fully, to invest in their own mental health, and to serve more people long-term. A writer who sells their book isn't selling out—they're valuing the hours, the vulnerability, and the truth poured into every page. A caregiver who earns a living wage isn't betraying their role—they're honoring it.

If you've ever felt guilty for charging, ask yourself: *Would I expect someone else to do this work for free?* If the answer is no, then why not extend that same respect to yourself?

Real-Life Examples

- *Sara*, 33, taught yoga and meditation. She loved her work but felt guilty charging for it. Her parents had instilled the belief that healing should be offered freely. When she raised her rates slightly, a client accused her of "selling spirituality." Sara almost quit. But after speaking with a mentor, she realized that sustainability was part of service. She created tiered pricing and offered scholarships—earning with integrity and compassion.
- *Nikhil*, 29, was a poet who performed at open mics. He often felt embarrassed asking for payment, believing art should be shared, not sold. But after struggling to afford rent, he began offering workshops and selling chapbooks. He wrote a poem called "The Price of Passion" that went viral—and helped others see that earning doesn't dilute art, it sustains it.

A Principle to Rise: The Principle of Worth-Aligned Income

Your work deserves compensation. The way to rise is to earn in alignment with your values. This is the Principle of Worth-Aligned Income.

Worth-Aligned Income means:

- Honor your energy exchange—your time matters.
- Use the "Fair Price Filter": Would I pay this for someone else's work?

- Detach income from morality.
- Create a money mantra: "I earn with integrity."
- Teach others how to treat your work–with clarity and boundaries.

Chapter 4
Boundaries Around Money

"I've learned that you can't be generous to others if you're constantly bankrupting yourself."

Oprah Winfrey

Money isn't just about spending and saving–it's also about relationships. How we talk about money, how we share it, and how we protect it can affect our peace of mind. That's why setting boundaries around money is so important. Boundaries help you stay clear, confident, and safe–especially when emotions, family, or expectations get involved.

Sometimes, people feel pressured to lend money they can't afford to lose. Or they feel guilty for saying no when someone asks for help. Others might overspend just to keep up with friends or avoid feeling left out. These situations can leave you feeling drained, resentful, or anxious. Boundaries are how you protect yourself from that.

Setting boundaries doesn't mean you're selfish–it means you're being responsible. It's okay to say:

- "I'm not in a position to lend right now."
- "I'd love to join, but it's not in my budget this month."
- "Let's talk openly about how we're splitting costs."

Real-Life Examples

- *Ananya*, 34, was the "go-to" person in her family for financial help. She lent money often, even when it hurt her own plans. She feared being seen as cold. But after a close cousin defaulted on a loan without acknowledgment, she felt betrayed. She created a lending policy: no loans without written terms. It was uncomfortable at first, but it taught her that love doesn't mean financial sacrifice.
- *Vikram*, 39, supported his siblings through college, weddings, and emergencies. He never said no. But when his own child's education fund ran low, he realized he'd been giving from an empty cup. He had honest conversations with his family and set new boundaries. It didn't break the bond–it strengthened it.

A Principle to Rise: The Principle of Financial Self-Respect

Boundaries build trust and clarity. The way to rise is to honor your limits with compassion. This is the Principle of Financial Self-Respect.

Financial Self-Respect means:

- Use the "Energy Exchange" test: Does this leave me empowered?
- Create a boundary script: "I'm not in a position to help financially."
- Prioritize your goals first.
- Remember: boundaries protect relationships, not destroy them.

Chapter 5
Financial Trauma and Recovery

"It always seems impossible until it's done."

Nelson Mandela

Financial trauma doesn't always come from numbers–it comes from betrayal, loss, and the silence that follows. It's the sinking feeling when someone you trusted disappears with your money. It's the sleepless nights after watching your savings vanish in the stock market. It's the shame, the confusion, and the quiet grief that no one talks about because "it's just money."

But it's not just money. It's your time. Your trust. Your effort. Your hope.

Maybe you lent a friend a large sum–because you believed in them, because they promised to return it, because you didn't think you needed a contract between friends. And now they won't take your calls. They've vanished, and you're left not only with financial loss, but emotional wreckage. You feel used. You feel foolish. You replay the moment you said yes, wondering how you didn't see it coming.

Or maybe you invested in the stock market–your first big step toward financial independence. You researched, you planned, you believed. And then the market crashed. You watched your hard-earned money disappear in days. You felt helpless. Angry. Embarrassed. You stopped checking your account. You stopped talking about it. You started doubting yourself.

These moments leave scars. Not just on your bank balance, but on your confidence. On your ability to trust others—and yourself.

But here's the truth: **you are not your financial trauma.** You are not the mistake, the loss, or the betrayal. You are the person who survived it. And you can recover.

Real-Life Examples

- *Sneha*, 29, grew up in a household where money was a constant source of fear. As an adult, she avoided budgeting, ignored bills, and felt paralyzed by financial decisions. After a panic attack at the ATM, she began therapy. She started small—checking her account once a week, tracking expenses with a friend. Slowly, the fear loosened its grip.
- *Aman*, 45, lost his business in a recession. He felt like a failure and avoided money conversations for years. When his daughter asked why he never talked about work, he broke down. That moment led him to financial counseling, where he processed the grief and began again—with humility and hope.
- Riya, 29, lent ₹1.5 lakh to a close friend who was going through a tough time. She didn't ask for paperwork—just trusted his word. At first, he promised to repay soon. Then he stopped replying to messages. Calls went unanswered. Months passed, and the friendship faded into silence. Riya wasn't just hurt financially—she felt deeply betrayed. It took her a long time to stop blaming herself. Eventually, she began journaling, set firmer boundaries, and now keeps all financial agreements in writing—even with people she loves.

- Sumit, 25, was the first in his family to earn a stable income. Relatives often asked for financial help, and he found it hard to say no. Over time, he drained her savings trying to meet everyone's expectations. When he finally set boundaries, he was called selfish. It hurt—but he stood firm. He now supports his family in ways that feel sustainable, and he's learned that protecting his financial health is not a betrayal—it's self-respect.
- Sameer, 31, received a call from someone claiming to be from his bank. They sounded professional and urgent. In a moment of panic, he shared his OTP. Within minutes, ₹85,000 was gone. He felt foolish and didn't tell anyone for weeks. Eventually, he reported the fraud, spoke to a counselor, and joined an online support group for scam victims. He now educates others about digital safety and has rebuilt his confidence.

A Principle to Rise: The Principle of Financial Healing

Money wounds need care. The way to rise is to treat financial trauma like emotional trauma. This is the Principle of Financial Healing.

Financial Healing means:

- Name the wound—journal your money memories.
- Use the "Safety First" approach—build buffers.
- Practice exposure therapy—engage gently with money tasks.
- Create a healing mantra: "I am safe. I am growing."
- Seek support—therapy, community, mentorship.

Chapter 6
Investing in Your Future Self

"Someone's sitting in the shade today because someone planted a tree a long time ago."

Warren Buffett

Investing isn't just about multiplying money–it's about multiplying possibility. It's the quiet, confident decision to believe in your future. For many, investing feels intimidating, reserved for the wealthy or the financially savvy. But the truth is: anyone can invest. Whether it's ₹500 a month or ₹50,000, investing is a way to say, "I trust myself to grow." It's not about chasing riches–it's about building resilience, freedom, and choice.

Real-Life Examples

- *Anjali*, 29, kept all her savings in a basic bank account. She feared losing money and didn't understand investing. After attending a free financial literacy workshop, she learned about mutual funds and started a SIP (Systematic Investment Plan) with ₹1,000/month. Over time, she saw her money grow and felt more confident making financial decisions.
- *Ramesh*, 45, ran a small business and never thought about retirement. A friend introduced him to Post Office Recurring

Deposits and Fixed Deposits. He started small, and now he has a safety net that gives him peace of mind and a sense of control over his future.

- *Tanya*, 34, was curious about the stock market but overwhelmed by jargon. She began by investing in index funds and reading beginner-friendly blogs. She didn't become a trader—but she became an investor. That shift changed how she saw herself: capable, informed, and in control.

A Principle to Rise: The Principle of Intentional Growth

Investing is a form of self-trust. The way to rise is to grow your money with clarity, consistency, and care. This is the Principle of Intentional Growth.

Intentional Growth means:

- **Start where you are** You don't need a fortune to begin. Even ₹500/month in a mutual fund builds momentum. The key is consistency, not quantity.
- **Know your options** Choose tools that match your comfort level and goals:
    - *Mutual Funds*: Professionally managed and diversified. SIPs (Systematic Investment Plans) help you invest monthly with discipline.
    - *Stock Market*: Higher risk, higher reward. Start with index funds or blue-chip stocks. Learn before you leap.
    - *Post Office RD (Recurring Deposit)*: Safe and reliable. Ideal for conservative savers who want fixed returns.
    - *Fixed Deposits (FDs)*: Guaranteed returns with flexible tenures. Great for short-term goals or emergency funds.

- **Match your goals to your tools** Use FDs for stability, mutual funds for long-term growth, and RDs for disciplined saving. Each tool serves a different emotional and financial purpose.
- **Learn before you leap** Read beginner guides, watch videos, or talk to a financial advisor. Financial literacy is emotional empowerment.
- **Track your emotional ROI** Investing isn't just about returns—it's about how it makes you feel: secure, hopeful, and free. Celebrate the confidence you gain, not just the numbers.

Part Seven

Dark Psychology: Protecting Your Mind from Manipulation

Chapter 1
Gaslighting: Reclaiming Your Reality

Gaslighting is when someone makes you question your memory, perception, or sanity. It's psychological warfare disguised as concern or logic.

It is one of the most subtle and damaging forms of emotional manipulation. It doesn't leave bruises, but it can fracture your sense of self. It happens when someone makes you doubt your own memory, feelings, or perception of reality. They twist facts, deny things they said, or make you feel "too sensitive" or "crazy" for reacting. Over time, you begin to question your own instincts, and that's exactly what the gaslighter wants–to control the narrative and keep you off balance.

Real-Life Example

- *Jeff*, 28, was told he was "too sensitive" every time he expressed discomfort. Over time, he stopped trusting his own feelings. Once he learned about gaslighting, he began journaling and validating his own emotions.
- Priya, 27 – The Relationship That Made Her Doubt Herself Priya was in a relationship where her partner constantly dismissed her feelings. If she brought up something hurtful he said, he'd reply, "I never said that. You're making it up." When she found messages that contradicted his story, he'd say, "You're reading too much into it." Over time, Priya

stopped trusting her own memory. She began apologizing for things she didn't do and questioning whether she was the problem. It wasn't until she spoke to a therapist that she realized she was being gaslit.

- Ramesh, 35 – Financial Gaslighting by a Business Partner Ramesh co-founded a small business with a friend. When profits started disappearing, his partner insisted, "You must have miscalculated. You always get confused with numbers." Even when Ramesh showed bank statements, his partner said, "You're being paranoid. You're imagining fraud." Ramesh began doubting his own judgment, until an accountant confirmed the missing funds. The gaslighting had masked financial manipulation.

- Aanya, 30 – Family Gaslighting Over Career Choices Aanya wanted to pursue art, but her parents constantly told her, "You're not talented enough. You'll regret this." When she expressed hurt, they said, "We're just being realistic. You're too emotional." Over time, Aanya stopped painting. She believed she was foolish for dreaming. Years later, she realized their "concern" was actually control—and she began reclaiming her creative voice.

- Kabir, 40 – Workplace Gaslighting Kabir's manager often changed deadlines without notice, then blamed Kabir for missing them. When Kabir pointed out the inconsistencies, the manager said, "You must have misunderstood. I never said that." Kabir started staying late, overworking, and second-guessing every email. The stress affected his health. Eventually, he documented everything and brought it to HR—only then did others admit they'd seen the same behavior.

Principle to Rise: Emotional Validation Trust your feelings. If something feels wrong, it deserves attention—even if others dismiss it.

Chapter 2
Love Bombing: When Affection Is a Trap

Love bombing feels like a dream at first. You're showered with compliments, gifts, constant messages, and promises of forever. It's intense, fast, and overwhelming–in a way that feels flattering. You might think, "*Wow, I've never been loved like this before.*" But that's the trap.

Love bombing isn't genuine affection–it's a tactic. It's used to gain control, build dependency, and blur boundaries. Once you're emotionally invested, the tone shifts. The attention fades. The praise turns into criticism. You're left confused, wondering what you did wrong, trying to earn back the love that was never real to begin with.

This pattern is common in toxic relationships, especially with narcissistic or controlling partners. It's not about love–it's about power.

Real-Life Examples

- Ishita, 25 - The Fairytale That Turned Cold When Ishita met Aarav, he was charming, attentive, and romantic. Within two weeks, he was calling her his soulmate, sending flowers daily, and texting her nonstop. She felt swept off her feet. But once she committed, things changed. He started criticizing her clothes, questioning her friends, and pulling away emotionally. When she asked what happened, he said,

"You're too needy." Ishita realized the affection was never about her—it was about control.

- Rohan, 32 – From Hero to Hostage Rohan met someone online who seemed perfect. She praised him constantly, said he was "the best man she'd ever met," and talked about marriage within a month. He felt seen and valued. But soon, she began guilt-tripping him for spending time with friends, accusing him of not caring enough. When he tried to set boundaries, she'd say, "After everything I've done for you?" Rohan felt trapped—like he owed her loyalty for the love she had bombed him with.
- Sana, 28 – The Boss Who Couldn't Let Go Sana's manager was overly complimentary when she joined the team. He praised her work, gave her special projects, and even invited her to exclusive events. She felt lucky. But when she started asserting herself, he became cold and dismissive. He'd say things like, "I thought you were different." The early praise had been a setup—once she stopped feeding his ego, the warmth disappeared.
- Mehul, 40 – Family Love with Strings Attached Mehul's older brother always showered him with gifts and praise during family gatherings. But whenever Mehul made a decision his brother didn't approve of—like changing jobs or setting boundaries—he'd withdraw, stop calling, and make passive-aggressive comments. Mehul realized the affection was conditional: it only flowed when he complied.

Principle to Rise: Slow Trust Let trust grow over time. Real love doesn't rush, it roots.

Chapter 3
The Silent Treatment: Weaponized Silence

The silent treatment is used to punish, control, or create anxiety. It's not about space–it's about power.

Silence can be peaceful. It can be healing. But when silence is used to punish, control, or create fear–it becomes a weapon. The silent treatment isn't about taking space to cool off or reflect. It's about power. It's about making someone feel invisible, uncertain, and desperate for connection.

When someone deliberately ignores you, refuses to respond, or shuts down communication without explanation, it creates emotional chaos. You start questioning yourself: *Did I do something wrong? Should I apologize? Are they angry?* That confusion is exactly what the silent treatment is designed to provoke. It's not a pause–it's a punishment.

Real-Life Example

- *Ritika*, 40, noticed her partner would go silent for days after arguments. She felt desperate for resolution. Once she understood the tactic, she stopped chasing and started setting boundaries.
- Ananya, 26 – The Relationship That Felt Like Walking on Glass Ananya's boyfriend would go silent for days after any disagreement. No texts. No calls. No explanation. When she tried to reach out, he'd say, "I just needed space." But it wasn't

space—it was control. She felt anxious, constantly trying to "fix" things, even when she hadn't done anything wrong. Over time, she realized his silence was a way to avoid accountability and keep her emotionally dependent.

- Vikram, 34 – The Cold Shoulder at Work Vikram's manager stopped acknowledging him after he questioned a team decision. Emails went unanswered. He was excluded from meetings. The silence wasn't professional—it was punitive. Vikram felt isolated and unsure of his standing. Eventually, he documented the behavior and spoke to HR, realizing that silence can be a form of workplace bullying.
- Meera, 40 – Family Silence That Hurt More Than Words Meera had a disagreement with her sister over a financial issue. Instead of talking it through, her sister stopped speaking to her entirely—for months. Family gatherings became tense. Meera felt guilt and confusion, even though she had tried to resolve things. The silence wasn't about healing—it was about control and emotional punishment.
- Aarav, 29 – Ghosted by a Friend Aarav shared something vulnerable with a close friend, expecting support. Instead, the friend disappeared. No replies. No explanation. Aarav kept replaying the moment, wondering if he'd said something wrong. The silence made him feel ashamed and abandoned. Later, he realized that true friends don't vanish when things get real—they show up.

Principle to Rise: Emotional Clarity Silence should bring peace, not punishment. Choose relationships that communicate, not confuse.

Chapter 4
Triangulation: Divide and Control

Triangulation involves bringing a third person into conflict to create jealousy, competition, or confusion.

It is a manipulation tactic where someone brings a third person into a conflict–not to resolve it, but to stir jealousy, create competition, or confuse the situation. It's a way to shift power, avoid accountability, and keep people off balance. Instead of addressing issues directly, the manipulator uses others as emotional weapons.

It might look like:

- Comparing you to someone else to make you feel inadequate
- Telling you what someone "really thinks" about you to spark insecurity
- Using a third person to relay messages instead of speaking to you directly
- Creating drama between people to stay in control of the narrative

Triangulation isn't about communication–it's about control. It divides people, erodes trust, and keeps the manipulator at the center of attention.

Real-Life Examples

- *Aman*, 25, noticed his friend constantly compared him to others to make him feel inferior. He realized it was a tactic to keep him insecure and dependent.
- Simran, 28 – The Jealous Partner Simran's boyfriend often mentioned how "cool" his female coworker was. He'd say things like, "She really understands me," or "She's so chill—unlike some people." Simran felt insecure and started questioning herself. When she brought it up, he said, "You're just being jealous." Over time, Simran realized he was using triangulation to make her feel small and dependent on his approval.
- Aditya, 35 – The Toxic Manager Aditya's manager never gave direct feedback. Instead, he'd say things like, "People on the team are starting to question your performance," or "I heard someone say you're not pulling your weight." Aditya didn't know who said it or if it was even true. The vague criticism made him anxious and isolated. The manager used triangulation to avoid direct confrontation and keep control through fear.
- Neha, 40 – Family Drama Neha's mother often told her, "Your sister thinks you're selfish," or "Your father agrees with me—you're too emotional." But when Neha spoke to her sister or father, they denied saying those things. Her mother was triangulating—using family members to manipulate Neha's emotions and make her feel guilty. It created tension and mistrust within the family.
- Kabir, 30 – Friendship Turned Competitive Kabir noticed his friend constantly compared him to another mutual friend: "You know, Raj always shows up on time," or "Raj's career is really taking off." It felt like Kabir was being pitted against

someone he cared about. The friend used triangulation to create competition and keep Kabir seeking approval.

Principle to Rise: Direct Connection Healthy relationships are built on clarity not comparison.

Chapter 5
Guilt-Tripping: Emotional Blackmail

Guilt-tripping uses your empathy against you. It's a way to control your decisions by making you feel responsible for someone else's emotions.

It is one of the most common forms of emotional manipulation–and one of the hardest to spot. It doesn't scream. It whispers. It shows up in phrases like *"After everything I've done for you..."* or *"I guess I just don't matter to you anymore."* It's not about open conflict–it's about quiet control.

Guilt-tripping works by making you feel responsible for someone else's emotions, even when you've done nothing wrong. It turns your boundaries into betrayal, your choices into selfishness, and your independence into abandonment. The goal isn't resolution–it's submission.

It's emotional blackmail disguised as love, concern, or sacrifice.

Real-Life Examples

- Tanya, 29 – The Mother Who Always Sacrificed Tanya wanted to move to another city for a better job. When she told her mother, she heard: "I gave up my whole life for you, and now you're leaving me?" Tanya felt torn. She knew her mother loved her, but the guilt made her question her decision. It wasn't a conversation–it was emotional pressure.

Tanya eventually realized that honoring her own growth didn't mean she was ungrateful.

- Arjun, 33 – The Friend Who Kept Score Arjun had a childhood friend who often said things like, "Remember when I helped you through that breakup? And now you can't even come to my party?" Every favor came with strings attached. Arjun started feeling obligated instead of connected. He realized the friendship was built on guilt, not mutual respect.
- Meera, 40 – The Partner Who Played the Victim Meera's partner would say, "If you really loved me, you wouldn't need space." Whenever she tried to set boundaries or take time for herself, he'd act hurt and withdrawn. She felt like she had to choose between her well-being and his approval. Over time, Meera saw that love shouldn't come with emotional ultimatums.
- Kabir, 36 – The Boss Who Used Loyalty as Leverage Kabir asked for a weekend off after months of overtime. His boss replied, "I thought you were committed to the team. Guess I was wrong." Kabir felt guilty, even though he had earned the break. The guilt wasn't about the job–it was about control.

Principle to Rise: Boundaried Compassion You can care deeply without being controlled. Empathy should empower not enslave.

Chapter 6
Projection: Their Feelings, Your Fault

Projection is when someone attributes their own flaws or emotions to you. It's a way to avoid accountability and shift blame.

It is when someone takes their own emotions like anger, guilt, insecurity, fear–and places them onto you. Instead of owning their feelings, they blame you for them. It's a defense mechanism, often unconscious, but it can be deeply damaging. You end up carrying emotions that aren't yours, apologizing for things you didn't do, and questioning your own behavior when the real issue isn't even about you.

It's like emotional hot-potato: they feel something uncomfortable, and instead of dealing with it, they toss it into your lap.

Projection can show up in relationships, families, workplaces–even friendships. It's not always loud or obvious. Sometimes it's subtle, wrapped in concern or criticism. But the pattern is clear: you're made to feel responsible for someone else's emotional mess.

Real-Life Examples

- *Rahul*, 37, was constantly accused of being "angry" by his partner–who was the one yelling. He realized he was absorbing someone else's emotional baggage.

- Rhea, 30 – The Insecure Partner Rhea's boyfriend constantly accused her of flirting, even though she was always respectful and loyal. He'd say things like, "You're always trying to get attention," or "I saw how you looked at that guy." Over time, Rhea started doubting herself. Later, she discovered he had been texting other women. His accusations were projections of his own guilt.
- Aman, 38 – The Defensive Manager Aman's boss often snapped at him during meetings, saying, "You're always so disorganized," even though Aman was known for his planning skills. Eventually, Aman realized the manager was overwhelmed and behind on his own tasks. Instead of admitting that, he projected his stress onto Aman to deflect attention.
- Nisha, 27 – The Controlling Parent Nisha's mother often said, "You're so selfish. You never think about anyone but yourself," whenever Nisha tried to set boundaries or make independent choices. But Nisha had spent years putting her family first. Her mother's words were projections of her own fear of losing control–not reflections of Nisha's behavior.
- Dev, 34 – The Friend Who Couldn't Own His Feelings Dev's friend accused him of being "too distant" and "not caring enough," right after Dev had spent weeks checking in and offering support. When Dev gently pointed this out, his friend said, "You're just trying to make me feel guilty." Dev realized his friend was projecting his own emotional neglect onto him.

Principle to Rise: Emotional Ownership You are not responsible for someone else's unresolved emotions. Own yours–return theirs.

Chapter 7
Mirroring: The Illusion of Compatibility

Mirroring is when someone copies your interests, values, or personality to gain trust. It feels like a soulmate—but it's often a strategy.

It is when someone reflects your interests, values, and personality back to you—not because they genuinely share them, but to create a false sense of connection. It feels magical at first. You meet someone who seems to "get" you instantly. They love the same music, share your dreams, and even finish your sentences. You think, *"Finally, someone who understands me."*

But mirroring isn't always authentic. In manipulative relationships, it's used to gain trust quickly, bypass emotional boundaries, and make you feel like you've found your perfect match. Once you're emotionally invested, the mask slips. The real person emerges—and they're nothing like the version they mirrored.

Mirroring is not compatibility. It's performance.

Real-Life Examples

- *Dev*, 34, met someone who seemed perfect—until he realized they were reflecting him, not revealing themselves.
- Aanya, 26 – The "Perfect" Date Aanya met someone through a dating app who seemed like her soulmate. He loved the same books, had the same political views, and even claimed to have childhood experiences that mirrored hers. She felt deeply

connected–until she noticed inconsistencies. He couldn't name the authors he claimed to love. His opinions changed depending on who he was around. Aanya realized he had mirrored her to win her trust, not because they were truly aligned.

- Rishi, 34 – The Business Partner Who Played Along Rishi started a creative venture with a colleague who seemed to share his passion for ethical business and slow growth. They talked about values, long-term vision, and staying grounded. But once money started coming in, the partner pushed for shortcuts, aggressive marketing, and profit over people. Rishi felt betrayed. The early "alignment" had been a strategy to get him on board.
- Meenal, 29 – The Friend Who Became a Mirror Meenal noticed that her new friend started dressing like her, using her phrases, and copying her social media style. At first, it felt flattering. But soon, Meenal felt like she was being studied–not supported. When she tried to express discomfort, the friend became defensive and distant. The friendship wasn't built on mutual respect–it was built on imitation.
- Kabir, 38 – The Manager Who Knew All the Right Words Kabir's new manager seemed emotionally intelligent, saying things like "I value transparency" and "Mental health matters here." But when Kabir opened up about burnout, the manager dismissed it as "excuses." Kabir realized the manager had mirrored progressive language to appear supportive–but didn't actually practice what he preached.

Principle to Rise: Authentic Connection

Real connection is built on truth, not tactics. Look for depth, not duplication.

Chapter 8
Breadcrumbing: Keeping You Hooked

Breadcrumbing is when someone gives you just enough attention to keep you interested but never enough to build a real connection. It's emotional manipulation through scarcity.

It's a trail of tiny crumbs: a late-night text, a flirty comment, a vague promise to meet up. It feels like something is *almost* happening, but it never really does. You're left waiting, hoping, checking your phone—and questioning your worth.

This behavior is often intentional. The person breadcrumbing you wants to keep you emotionally available without committing. It's not about love or friendship—it's about control. They want the comfort of knowing you're there, without the responsibility of showing up for you.

Breadcrumbing can happen in romantic relationships, friendships, even professional settings. It's confusing, draining, and deeply unfair.

Real-Life Examples

- *Tanya*, 27, kept receiving vague texts and promises from someone who never showed up. She realized she was being strung along.
- Isha, 27 – The Flirty Ex Who Never Left After breaking up, Isha's ex kept texting her every few weeks: "Thinking of you,"

or "Miss our late-night talks." But whenever she suggested meeting or having a real conversation, he'd disappear. She felt stuck—unable to move on, yet never truly reconnecting. The crumbs kept her emotionally hooked, even though the relationship was over.

- Aarav, 31 – The Boss Who Dangled Promises Aarav's manager often said things like, "You're next in line for promotion," or "Big things are coming your way." But months passed with no progress, no feedback, and no clarity. Aarav kept working harder, hoping the vague praise would turn into real opportunity. It never did. The breadcrumbs were about motivation—not actual growth.
- Neha, 25 – The Friend Who Only Reached Out When Lonely Neha had a friend who rarely made plans but would suddenly message her when feeling down: "You're the only one who gets me." Neha would drop everything to support her. But once the friend felt better, she'd vanish again. Neha realized she was being emotionally breadcrumbed—used for comfort, not connection.
- Rishi, 34 – The Crush That Never Became More Rishi met someone who seemed interested—liking his posts, replying to stories, sending occasional flirty texts. But every time he tried to make plans, they'd say, "I'm super busy right now, maybe soon." This went on for months. Rishi felt confused and frustrated. The attention was real, but the intention wasn't.

Principle to Rise: Full Presence You deserve consistency, not crumbs. Walk away from half-hearted energy.

Part Eight

Office & Everyday Politics: Navigating the Invisible Games

Chapter 1
The Gossip Trap: When Words Become Weapons

Gossip is rarely innocent. It's often a tool to bond, exclude, or manipulate. It creates alliances but also divides.

Real-Life Examples

- *Ravi*, 32, noticed his coworkers bonded over mocking others. He joined in to fit in until he became the target. He learned to step back and build trust through action, not whispers.
- Priya, 24 – The Office Whisper Network, Priya had just joined a new company and quickly became friendly with a few coworkers. One day, she overheard them gossiping about another colleague, saying she was "lazy" and "only got promoted because of favoritism." Priya didn't know the full story, but the comments shaped her opinion. Months later, she worked directly with that colleague and realized she was one of the most hardworking people on the team. The gossip had poisoned her perception before she even had a chance to form her own.
- Kabir, 36 – The Family Divide, Kabir's aunt told him that his cousin had been speaking negatively about him behind his back. Hurt and confused, Kabir distanced himself. Later, he found out the cousin had said nothing of the sort–the aunt

had misinterpreted a comment and exaggerated it. The damage was done. A close relationship was strained over words that were never truly spoken.

- Meenal, 30 – The Friendship That Turned Sour, Meenal confided in a friend about her struggles with anxiety. A few weeks later, she heard from someone else that her friend had shared her story, saying Meenal was "too emotional" and "always dramatic." Meenal felt betrayed. The gossip turned her vulnerability into a punchline, and the friendship never recovered.

Principle to Rise: Speak with Integrity: Words build reputations– yours and others'. Use them wisely.

Chapter 2
Favoritism: The Unspoken Hierarchy

In many workplaces, merit doesn't always win relationships do. Favoritism is rarely announced—but it's always felt. It's the quiet tilt in someone's tone, the extra attention given to one person, the invisible ladder that some seem to climb effortlessly while others are stuck at the bottom. Whether in families, workplaces, classrooms, or social circles, favoritism creates an unspoken hierarchy. And when you're not the favorite, you feel it in every overlooked idea, every missed opportunity, every subtle exclusion.

Favoritism isn't always malicious. Sometimes it's unconscious. But its impact is real. It breeds resentment, insecurity, and division. It tells people, *"You're not enough,"* without ever saying it out loud.

Real-Life Examples

- Niharika, 27 – The Workplace Star System Niharika worked diligently, but her manager consistently favored another colleague—offering praise, opportunities, and visibility. Niharika felt invisible and undervalued.

  Solution: She began documenting her contributions and requested regular one-on-one check-ins with her manager to discuss her goals and progress. By calmly presenting her achievements and asking for feedback, she shifted the dynamic from passive frustration to active advocacy. She also sought mentorship outside her team to build support and visibility.

- Zaid, 35 – The Family Divide In Zaid's family, his younger sister was always praised and prioritized, while Zaid's efforts were often dismissed. When he voiced his hurt, his parents denied any favoritism.

  Solution: Zaid stopped seeking validation from his parents and focused on building emotional boundaries. He began expressing his needs clearly–without guilt–and spent more time with people who appreciated him without comparison. He also started family conversations around fairness, not blame, which helped shift the tone over time.

- Tanvi, 31 – The Teacher's Pet Dynamic In college, Tanvi noticed her professor gave one student extra attention and leniency, while others were held to stricter standards. Her own requests for support were brushed off.

  Solution: Tanvi approached the professor with a respectful email outlining her concerns and requesting equal access to feedback and resources. She also formed a study group with classmates who felt similarly, creating a support system that helped them advocate together. Over time, the professor became more mindful of how they distributed attention.

- Harsh, 39 – The Friend Who Played Favorites Harsh was part of a friend group, but one person always got the emotional support and inside jokes. Harsh felt like a backup friend, not a real one.

  Solution: Harsh had an honest conversation with the group, expressing how the dynamic made him feel excluded. He didn't accuse–he shared. Some friends were surprised and made an effort to include him more intentionally. Harsh also began investing in friendships where he felt equally valued, rather than chasing approval from those who didn't reciprocate.

Principle to Rise: Value Yourself First: Don't wait for someone to notice you. Make your value visible.

Chapter 3
Credit Theft: When Your Work Isn't Yours

Credit theft happens when someone takes recognition for your ideas, your effort, or your achievements–without giving you the credit you deserve. It's not just frustrating; it's demoralizing. You put in the time, the creativity, the sweat–and someone else walks away with the applause.

This kind of behavior can show up in workplaces, group projects, families, and even friendships. Sometimes it's subtle, like someone repeating your idea louder in a meeting. Other times, it's blatant–like your name being left off a shared accomplishment. Either way, it chips away at your confidence and makes you question your value.

Signs of Credit Theft

- Your ideas are repeated by others without acknowledgment
- You're excluded from praise or recognition in group efforts
- Someone else takes ownership of your work or contributions
- You feel invisible despite doing the heavy lifting
- You're told to "let it go" when you ask for credit

Real-Life Examples

- Charvi, 29 – The Invisible Contributor Charvi spent weeks preparing a presentation for her team. Her manager presented it to leadership without mentioning her name. When the project was praised, Charvi sat in silence while others took the credit.

Solution: Charvi followed up with her manager privately and respectfully said, "I'd appreciate being acknowledged for my work in future presentations." She also began adding her name to shared documents and emails to establish visibility. Over time, her manager became more mindful, and Charvi's contributions were recognized more consistently.

- Danish, 37 – The Idea That Wasn't His Anymore During a brainstorming session, Danish suggested a new marketing strategy. A colleague later pitched the same idea to leadership, claiming it as their own. Danish felt betrayed and unsure how to respond without sounding petty.

  Solution: Danish documented his original idea and calmly brought it up in a follow-up meeting: "I'm glad the team liked the strategy–I'd love to share how I envisioned it evolving." By reclaiming ownership without confrontation, he re-established his role in the project and earned respect from others.

- Sneha, 33 – The Family Project That Got Rewritten Sneha helped organize a family event, handling logistics, budgeting, and planning. But when relatives praised the outcome, her sibling said, "It was a team effort–we all chipped in," despite doing very little. Sneha felt erased.

  Solution: Sneha didn't argue publicly. Instead, she spoke to her sibling privately and said, "I felt hurt when my work wasn't acknowledged. I need that recognition to feel respected." She also started setting clearer roles in future projects to avoid blurred boundaries.

- Arman, 40 – The Group Project Ghost In a professional workshop, Arman contributed heavily to a group assignment. When the final report was submitted, his name was missing from the credits. The team lead brushed it off as a "formatting error."

  Solution: Arman addressed it directly but professionally: "I noticed my name wasn't included–can we correct that before submission?" He also kept records of his contributions and began advocating for clearer authorship in collaborative work. His assertiveness helped prevent future oversights.

Principle to Rise: Own Your Voice: Document your work. Defend your impact. Don't disappear.

Chapter 4
Passive Aggression: The Smile with a Sting

Passive aggression hides hostility behind politeness. It's sarcasm, silence, or subtle sabotage.

It is the art of expressing anger or resentment without ever saying it directly. It's the compliment that feels like a jab, the silence that speaks volumes, the "just kidding" that cuts too deep. It's a smile that hides frustration, and a tone that says *"I'm fine"* when everything else says *"I'm not."*

Unlike open conflict, passive aggression is subtle. It's designed to avoid confrontation while still delivering emotional discomfort. You're left confused, second-guessing yourself, and wondering if you're overreacting. But you're not. Passive aggression is real—and it's a form of emotional manipulation.

Real-Life Examples

- *Megha*, 27, had a teammate who "forgot" to include her in emails and meetings. She addressed it directly—and the behavior stopped.
- Ira, 28 – The Roommate Who "Forgot" Ira's roommate often "forgot" to do shared chores, even after agreeing to a schedule. When Ira reminded her, she'd say, "Wow, you're really particular about things, aren't you?" with a smile. Ira felt dismissed and disrespected.

Solution: Ira stopped engaging in vague reminders and instead created a clear, written chore chart. She also addressed the behavior directly: "When you say things like that, it feels like you're mocking my effort. Can we talk about what's not working for you?" The clarity helped shift the dynamic from passive to honest.

- Rehan, 36 – The Manager Who Praised with a Twist Rehan's manager often said things like, "You finally got it right—took long enough," or "Nice job, for once." The words sounded like praise, but the tone stung. Rehan felt demoralized and unsure how to respond.

  Solution: Rehan began documenting his work and asking for specific feedback: "I'd love to know what worked well in this project so I can build on it." By steering the conversation toward constructive dialogue, he reduced the space for passive digs and reinforced his professionalism.

- Kavya, 31 – The Friend Who Used Sarcasm as a Shield Whenever Kavya shared good news, her friend would say things like, "Must be nice to have everything handed to you," or "Wow, some of us are still struggling." It was always followed by, "I'm just joking." But it didn't feel like a joke.

  Solution: Kavya addressed it gently but firmly: "I know you say you're joking, but those comments hurt. I'd rather we celebrate each other without sarcasm." Her honesty created space for a more respectful friendship—or revealed who wasn't willing to change.

Principle to Rise: Call It Out Calmly: You don't need to fight, just name the behavior. Clarity is power.

Chapter 5
Backstabbing:
The Betrayal Behind Your Back

Backstabbing is one of the most painful forms of betrayal. It's not a fight–it's a quiet attack when your guard is down. It happens behind closed doors, in whispered conversations, or through subtle sabotage. You trust someone, confide in them, support them–and they use that trust against you. The worst part? You often find out too late.

Backstabbing isn't just about gossip or lies. It's about broken loyalty. It leaves you questioning your judgment, your relationships, and sometimes even your self-worth. But recognizing it is the first step toward reclaiming your power.

Real-Life Examples

- Sanaya, 30 – The Colleague Who Took Credit and Cut Corners Sanaya collaborated with a coworker on a major project. She shared ideas, helped with execution, and trusted they were working as a team. But when the project was presented, her coworker took full credit and even implied Sanaya had contributed very little.

  Solution: Sanaya calmly addressed the issue with her manager, presenting her documented contributions and emails. She also began setting clearer boundaries in future collaborations–keeping records, clarifying roles, and ensuring her name was attached to her work. Her professionalism helped restore her credibility and protect her from future sabotage.

- Raghav, 38 – The Friend Who Shared Secrets Raghav confided in a close friend about a personal issue. Weeks later, he found out that same friend had shared his story with others, twisting the details and mocking him behind his back. Raghav felt humiliated and betrayed.

  Solution: Raghav confronted the friend directly, expressing how deeply the betrayal had hurt him. He didn't argue–he simply stated the facts and walked away. He chose to distance himself from the friendship and began surrounding himself with people who respected his privacy and vulnerability.

- Iqra, 33 – The Team Lead Who Undermined Her Iqra was up for a promotion and had strong performance reviews. But her team lead quietly told upper management that she was "not ready" and "too emotional under pressure," despite no evidence of this. Iqra only found out after being passed over for the role.

  Solution: Iqra requested a meeting with HR and shared her track record, feedback from peers, and examples of her leadership. She also asked for transparency in future evaluations. Her assertiveness led to a reevaluation of her candidacy–and a promotion months later.

- Veer, 41 – The Relative Who Played Both Sides Veer was caught in a family conflict where one relative pretended to support him, but secretly fueled drama by sharing his words out of context with others. The result? Misunderstandings, tension, and broken trust.

  Solution: Veer stopped confiding in that relative and began communicating directly with others involved. He clarified what he had actually said and chose to disengage from gossip-driven dynamics. His honesty helped rebuild trust with some family members—and revealed who wasn't safe to trust.

Principle to Rise: Guard Your Vulnerability: Not everyone deserves your truth. Share wisely.

Chapter 6
Sabotage: When Success Is Threatening

Some people feel threatened by others' growth. They may subtly block opportunities, spread doubt, or delay progress.

It isn't always loud or obvious. Sometimes, it's a quiet resistance to your growth. It shows up when your success makes someone uncomfortable–when your progress feels like a threat to their ego, status, or control. Instead of celebrating you, they undermine you. Instead of supporting you, they subtly block your path.

Sabotage can come from colleagues, friends, family–even mentors. It often hides behind politeness, vague criticism, or "helpful" advice that leads you off track. It's not about your failure–it's about their fear of your success.

Real-Life Examples

- Nupur, 32 – The Colleague Who Delayed Her Progress Nupur was leading a high-stakes project and relied on a teammate for key data. That teammate consistently missed deadlines, gave incomplete information, and then blamed Nupur for the delays. When the project faltered, Nupur was held responsible.

  Solution: Nupur began documenting every request and response, creating a clear timeline of her efforts. She looped in her manager early and requested support to reassign critical tasks. Her transparency protected her reputation and exposed the pattern of sabotage.

- Ayaan, 39 – The Friend Who Doubted Every Win When Ayaan launched his startup, his longtime friend kept saying things like, "Are you sure this is sustainable?" or "Don't get your hopes up too high." Instead of encouragement, he received constant doubt and subtle discouragement.

  Solution: Ayaan stopped sharing his milestones with that friend and began surrounding himself with people who celebrated his growth. He realized that not everyone is meant to walk beside you when you level up—and that's okay.

- Roshni, 28 – The Mentor Who Shifted the Spotlight Roshni was selected to speak at a major industry event. Her mentor, who had previously supported her, suddenly began questioning her readiness and suggested she let someone else take the stage "for the team." Roshni felt confused and betrayed.

  Solution: Roshni respectfully declined the suggestion and stood firm in her opportunity. She later found a new mentor who genuinely supported her growth. She learned that real mentorship lifts you up—not holds you back.

- Devansh, 36 – The Manager Who Withheld Opportunities Devansh consistently exceeded targets, but his manager never nominated him for leadership programs. When he asked why, the manager said, "You're doing great where you are—why change that?" Devansh realized his growth was being quietly blocked.

  Solution: Devansh began networking outside his department and applied directly for development programs. He also sought feedback from other leaders and built visibility beyond his manager's gatekeeping. Eventually, he transitioned to a role where his growth was supported.

Principle to Rise: Build Multiple Bridges: Don't rely on one gatekeeper. Expand your network.

Chapter 7
Emotional Manipulation: The Guilt Game

Emotional manipulation is when someone uses guilt, fear, or obligation to control your behavior. It's not about open conflict–it's about subtle pressure. The guilt game is one of the most common tactics: making you feel responsible for someone else's emotions, even when you've done nothing wrong.

It sounds like: "After everything I've done for you..." "I guess I just don't matter to you anymore." "If you really cared, you'd do this for me."

These phrases aren't about love or concern–they're about control. The manipulator wants you to feel bad so you'll give in, stay quiet, or change your decisions. Over time, you start second-guessing yourself, apologizing for things you didn't do, and sacrificing your own needs to avoid conflict.

Real-Life Examples

- Ayesha, 30 – The Parent Who Guilt-Tripped Every Boundary Ayesha wanted to move to a new city for a job opportunity. When she told her mother, she heard: "I gave up everything for you, and now you're leaving me?" Ayesha felt torn between her dreams and her mother's disappointment.

  Solution: Ayesha gently but firmly said, "I love you, and I'm grateful for everything you've done. But I need to make choices that are right for my future." She also set boundaries around emotional conversations and began seeking support from friends who encouraged her growth.

- Manav, 38 – The Partner Who Played the Victim Whenever Manav tried to take time for himself–whether to rest, work, or see friends–his partner would say, "I guess I'm just not important to you anymore." Manav felt guilty and often canceled plans to avoid conflict.

  Solution: Manav started recognizing the pattern and responded with clarity: "I care about you deeply, but taking time for myself doesn't mean I'm abandoning you." He suggested couples counseling to build healthier communication. The guilt began to lose its grip.

- Ritu, 27 – The Friend Who Kept Score Ritu had a friend who constantly reminded her of past favors: "Remember when I helped you move? And now you can't even come to my party?" Every interaction felt transactional.

  Solution: Ritu stopped engaging in guilt-based conversations and began setting emotional boundaries. She said, "I appreciate your support in the past, but I don't want our friendship to feel like a debt." The friendship either evolved–or revealed its limits.

- Arvind, 41 – The Boss Who Used Loyalty as Leverage Arvind asked for a weekend off after months of overtime. His boss replied, "I thought you were committed to the team. Guess I was wrong." Arvind felt guilty, even though he had earned the break.

  Solution: Arvind calmly responded, "I've given my best consistently, and taking time off is part of staying balanced. I'm still committed." He also began documenting his hours and contributions to protect himself from future emotional pressure.

Principle to Rise: Boundaries Over Approval: You're not selfish for protecting your energy. You're smart.

Chapter 8
The Politics of Praise: Flattery with Strings

Not all praise is genuine. Sometimes it's used to manipulate, distract, or gain favor.

Praise is supposed to uplift, affirm, and celebrate. But when it's used strategically–attached to expectations, manipulation, or hidden agendas–it becomes a tool for control. This is the politics of praise: when compliments aren't given freely, but as currency. You're praised not for who you are, but for what someone wants from you.

Flattery with strings often sounds like admiration, but it feels transactional. It's the boss who compliments your work right before asking you to stay late. The friend who gushes about your generosity, then asks for a favor. The partner who praises your strength, only to guilt you into silence. It's not about appreciation–it's about positioning.

Real-Life Examples

- Sakshi, 31 – The Manager Who Praised with a Catch Sakshi's manager often said things like, "You're the most reliable person on the team–I know I can count on you," right before assigning her extra work. The praise felt good at first, but over time, Sakshi realized it was being used to justify overloading her.

Solution: Sakshi began responding with boundaries: "I appreciate the trust, but I'm at capacity right now. Can we revisit this next week?" She also started tracking her workload and advocating for fair distribution. The praise lost its power when she stopped letting it override her limits.

- Imran, 38 – The Friend Who Complimented to Control Imran had a friend who often said, "You're the only one I can count on–you're so generous," right before asking for favors that felt one-sided. When Imran hesitated, the friend would say, "I thought you were different."

  Solution: Imran recognized the pattern and began setting firmer boundaries: "I care about you, but I can't always be available. Let's find a way that works for both of us." He stopped letting praise guilt him into overextending and started valuing mutual respect over flattery.

- Neelam, 34 – The Partner Who Used Compliments to Silence Neelam's partner often said, "You're so strong–I admire how you never complain," whenever she tried to express frustration. The praise was used to discourage vulnerability and keep her quiet.

  Solution: Neelam responded with honesty: "Being strong doesn't mean I don't feel things. I need space to express myself too." She began asserting her emotional needs and challenged the idea that praise should come at the cost of authenticity.

- Raghav, 40 – The Mentor Who Played Favorites Raghav's mentor frequently praised him in front of others: "Raghav's the future of this company." But privately, the mentor discouraged him from applying for leadership roles, saying, "Let's not rush–you're too valuable where you are." The praise was a leash, not a ladder.

Solution: Raghav began seeking feedback from other leaders and applied for roles independently. He realized that praise without progress is a form of control. By stepping outside the mentor's shadow, he reclaimed his growth.

Principle to Rise: Decode the Compliment: Ask like What's behind the praise? Is it appreciation or expectation?

Chapter 9
The Exit Strategy:
When It's Time to Walk Away

Sometimes, the best move is to leave. Toxic environments don't always change—and staying can cost your peace.

Sometimes, the most powerful move isn't fixing the situation—it's leaving it. The exit strategy isn't about giving up. It's about choosing yourself. It's the moment you realize that staying is costing you more than it's giving. Whether it's a toxic relationship, a draining job, or a friendship that's turned into emotional labor, walking away can be the most courageous act of self-respect.

Leaving doesn't mean you failed. It means you've outgrown the space that no longer nurtures you. It's not about revenge or drama—it's about peace.

Real-Life Examples

- Tara, 33 – The Relationship That Kept Her Small Tara had been in a relationship for five years. Her partner constantly dismissed her goals, mocked her ambitions, and made her feel guilty for wanting more. She kept hoping things would change, but they didn't. She realized she was shrinking to stay loved.

  Solution: Tara made a quiet, firm decision to leave. She moved out, leaned on her support system, and began therapy to rebuild her confidence. It wasn't easy—but it was necessary. Today, she's thriving in a space where her voice is heard and her dreams are honored.

- Adil, 40 – The Job That Drained His Soul Adil worked in a high-paying corporate role, but the environment was toxic. His ideas were ignored, his boundaries were violated, and his mental health was deteriorating. He stayed for the paycheck—until he realized the cost was too high.

  Solution: Adil created a financial cushion, updated his resume, and began networking quietly. Within months, he transitioned to a smaller company that valued his input and respected his time. The exit wasn't impulsive—it was strategic. And it changed his life.

- Naina, 28 – The Friendship That Became One-Sided Naina had a friend who only reached out when she needed something. Emotional support, favors, validation—but never reciprocation. Naina felt drained and unseen, but feared being "mean" if she walked away.

  Solution: Naina stopped initiating contact and let the silence speak. She didn't make a dramatic exit—she simply stopped overextending. She invested her energy into friendships that felt mutual and nourishing. Her peace returned when she stopped chasing approval.

- Raghav, 36 – The Family Dynamic That Wasn't Safe Raghav grew up in a family where emotional manipulation was normalized. Every boundary he set was met with guilt, shame, or silence. He tried for years to "fix" the relationship—but it only hurt more.

- Solution: Raghav chose limited contact. He stopped explaining himself and started protecting his emotional space.

He built a chosen family of friends and mentors who respected him. Walking away didn't mean abandoning love—it meant choosing a healthier version of it.

Principle to Rise: Choose Peace Over Proximity: You're not obligated to stay loyal to what harms you. Protecting your mental and emotional health is not selfish—it's essential.

Part Nine

Myths That Hold You Back

Chapter 1
"Small City, Small Dreams"

The Myth

"You earn less in a small city, but it's enough. Big cities are too expensive and too fast. Stay where you are–it's safer."

This is one of the most common myths whispered in middle-class Indian households. It's disguised as care, but often rooted in fear. The idea is simple: don't dream too big, don't move too far, and don't risk too much. But what they rarely tell you is that **big cities don't just cost more–they offer more**.

The Truth

Yes, metro cities like Delhi, Mumbai, Bengaluru, and Hyderabad come with higher living costs. But they also come with **higher salaries, better exposure, global networks, and faster growth**. The opportunities are not just more–they're bigger. And if you're willing to stretch, the rewards are exponential.

Real-Life Example:

Take **Ravi**, a graphic designer from a Tier-3 town in Haryana. He was earning ₹18,000/month working for a local print shop. His family discouraged him from moving to Delhi, saying, "Rent alone will eat your salary." But Ravi took the leap. Within six months, he was freelancing for startups and earning ₹60,000/month. Within two years, he was working remotely for a Singapore-based firm, making ₹1.2 lakh/month.

The same skills. The same person. Just a different city—and a different mindset.

What Keeps Us Stuck

- Fear of failure
- Pressure to conform
- Emotional blackmail ("Who will take care of us?")
- Lack of exposure to what's possible

But here's the truth: **comfort zones don't create legends**. They create routines. And routines don't rise.

The Shift

You don't have to abandon your roots to grow—you just have to **expand your reach**. Moving to a metro city isn't about rejecting your hometown. It's about choosing growth over stagnation.

If you're from a small town, you already know how to hustle. You've learned to make the most of limited resources. That grit will serve you well in any city. Don't let fear disguised as tradition hold you back.

Closing Reflection

Your first step might be scary. It might be lonely. But it will be worth it. The myth says "stay small." The truth says "start small—but don't stay there."

You were not born to fit in. You were born to rise.

Chapter 2
"Money Isn't Needed to Help Others"

The Myth

"You don't need money to help people. Just be kind."

This sounds noble—but it's incomplete. Kindness is powerful, yes. But **money amplifies impact**. Society often romanticizes poverty, as if being broke makes you morally superior. But the truth is, **you can do more good when you have more to give**.

The Truth

Money isn't the enemy—it's a tool. With wealth, you can fund education, support families, build shelters, and create jobs. You can help quietly or publicly, but your reach multiplies when your resources grow.

Real-Life Example:

Anita Dongre, a fashion designer, didn't just build a brand—she built a movement. With her success, she launched initiatives to support rural artisans, especially women. Her financial power became a force for social change.

Compare that to someone who wants to help but can't afford to. The intention is there—but the impact is limited.

The Shift

Don't feel guilty for wanting to earn more. Wanting wealth doesn't make you greedy–it makes you capable. The more you grow, the more you can give.

Chapter 3
Never Argue with Elders

The Myth

"Respect your elders–never question them."

This belief runs deep in Indian households. Elders are often treated as unquestionable authorities, even when their behavior is harmful. The idea that age automatically earns respect can lead to silence in the face of manipulation, humiliation, or even abuse.

Children and young adults are taught to "adjust," "stay quiet," or "not talk back." But respect should never mean submission. Age doesn't excuse cruelty. Silence doesn't protect peace–it protects patterns.

The Truth

If someone crosses a boundary, speak up. Whether it's a parent, uncle, teacher, or elder, your voice matters. Respect is not blind obedience–it's mutual dignity. You are allowed to challenge what hurts you. You are allowed to protect yourself.

Real-Life Example 1: Riya, College Student

Riya, a journalism student, was constantly belittled by her grandfather for not choosing engineering. He mocked her career choice, called her "naive," and dismissed her achievements. For years, she stayed silent, fearing it would be "disrespectful" to speak up. Eventually, she confronted him–with calm but firm words. She explained her goals and demanded basic respect. The ridicule stopped. Her confidence grew. Her silence had protected his ego—but her voice protected her future.

Real-Life Example 2: Meenal, 19-Year-Old Student

Meenal had always looked up to her mother's cousin, who was in his late 30s and often treated as a respected elder in the family. After she turned 21, he began sending her inappropriate messages and explicit photos, suggesting they meet privately and asking her out. Initially shocked and confused, Meenal feared that speaking up would cause family conflict or be seen as disrespectful. But instead of staying silent, she took a bold step—she shared everything with her mother and confronted him directly. Her mother stood firmly by her side. The cousin was confronted by the family and distanced from future gatherings. Meenal's courage not only protected herself—it sent a clear message that boundaries matter, regardless of age or relation.

The Shift

Respect is mutual. If someone disrespects you, age doesn't shield them from accountability. You are allowed to speak your truth—even when it's uncomfortable. You are allowed to protect your dignity—even when it challenges tradition.

Silence may feel safer in the moment, but it often leads to long-term suffering. Your voice is not rebellion—it's self-respect.

Chapter 4
Be Satisfied with What You Have

The Myth

"Be content. Don't be greedy."

On the surface, this sounds like wisdom. But in practice, it's often used to suppress ambition—especially in middle-class households across India. Children are taught to be grateful for what they have, not to dream too big, and to avoid "risking everything" for something uncertain.

This mindset is passed down with phrases like:

- "Why chase more? You already have enough."
- "Don't be greedy—learn to adjust."
- "People like us don't live like that."
- "You'll lose everything trying to get more."

But satisfaction, when weaponized, becomes a cage. It teaches people to settle too soon, to stop evolving, and to fear their own potential.

The Truth

You can be grateful and still want more. Wanting a better life isn't greed—it's vision. Dreaming big doesn't mean you're ungrateful—it means you're alive.

Ambition doesn't cancel gratitude—it deepens it. It says, "I honor what I have, and I believe I can build more." Growth requires hunger. And hunger is not a flaw—it's fuel.

Real-Life Example 1: Sundar Pichai, CEO of Google

Born in Chennai to a modest family, Sundar Pichai could have settled for a comfortable life in India. But he pursued education abroad, took risks, and climbed through the ranks of Silicon Valley. Today, he leads one of the world's most influential tech companies. His story isn't about greed—it's about growth, vision, and relentless curiosity.

Real-Life Example 2: Kalpana Saroj, Entrepreneur

Born into poverty and married off at 12, Kalpana faced abuse, discrimination, and despair. She could have accepted her fate—but she didn't. She rebuilt her life, started small businesses, and eventually took over Kamani Tubes, turning it into a multi-million-dollar company. Her rise wasn't about dissatisfaction—it was about refusing to be defined by limitations.

Real-Life Example 3: Nawazuddin Siddiqui, Actor

Nawazuddin worked as a watchman and chemist before entering films. For years, he played minor roles and faced rejection. He could have settled—but he kept pushing. Today, he's one of India's most respected actors, known for his depth and authenticity. His journey proves that wanting more doesn't mean forgetting where you came from—it means honoring it by rising.

Real-Life Example 4: Ritu, 35-Year-Old Homemaker Turned Entrepreneur

Ritu spent a decade as a homemaker in Ludhiana. She loved her family—but felt a creative hunger she couldn't ignore. She started baking from home, then launched a small business. Today, she runs a thriving bakery and teaches workshops to other women. Her story shows that satisfaction and ambition can coexist—and that growth can begin at any stage.

The Shift

Don't let "satisfaction" become a cage. You're allowed to want more. You're allowed to rise.

Gratitude is a foundation—not a ceiling. You can appreciate what you have and still build something greater. You don't owe anyone smallness. You owe yourself expansion.

Chapter 5
Marriage Is the Ultimate Goal

The Myth

"For women, marriage is the destination. For men, it's the milestone."

This belief is deeply embedded in Indian society. From a young age, girls are conditioned to believe that their ultimate achievement is to become a good wife. Boys are told that marriage is something to consider once they've settled professionally. The pressure is relentless–subtle in some families, overt in others.

If you're unmarried past a certain age, especially as a woman, society begins to whisper louder:

- "You're late."
- "How will you survive in old age?"
- "Who will take care of you?"
- "Don't you want stability?"
- "People will think something is wrong with you."

These aren't just questions–they're fears disguised as concern. They're designed to push people into relationships they may not be ready for, or worse, not meant for.

The Truth

Marriage should be a choice, not a compulsion. You are not incomplete without a partner. You are not late if you're single. Your worth is not tied to your marital status.

You can build a life full of love, purpose, and connection—whether or not you ever marry. Companionship is beautiful, but it's not the only path to fulfillment. Your dreams, your work, your friendships, your self-respect—they all count. You don't need a spouse to validate your existence.

The Fear Society Plants

- Loneliness in old age: "Who will be there for you?"
- Social exclusion: "You won't be invited to family events the same way."
- Financial insecurity: "You need a partner to share responsibilities."
- Moral judgment: "People will think something is wrong with you."

But companionship doesn't have to come from marriage. It can come from community, chosen family, friendships, and self-built support systems. Financial independence is possible. Emotional fulfillment is possible. And dignity is non-negotiable.

Real-Life Example 1: Gauri, Entrepreneur

Gauri, a 34-year-old founder from Pune, faced constant pressure to "settle down." Her relatives warned her: "You'll regret this later. Who will take care of you?" But Gauri chose to build her startup first. Today, she employs over 50 people, mentors young women, and lives a life filled with purpose. She's single—and thriving. Her life is full, with or without a husband.

Real-Life Example 2: Dr. Vandana Shiva, Environmental Activist

Dr. Shiva never married. Instead, she devoted her life to environmental justice, food sovereignty, and women's rights. She's traveled the world, written books, and built movements. Her legacy is global. Her life proves that impact doesn't require a spouse–it requires vision.

Real-Life Example 3: Dia Mirza, Actor and Environmentalist

Dia Mirza married for the first time at age 39. Her decision was thoughtful, grounded in mutual respect and shared values. She has spoken openly about how her later-in-life marriage allowed her to enter the relationship with clarity and emotional maturity. Today, she balances her personal life with activism and public service.

Real-Life Example 4: Ramesh and Kavita, Couple from Bengaluru

Ramesh, a software engineer, married Kavita, a school principal, when both were in their early 40s. It was the first marriage for both. They met through a shared interest in literature and community work. Their relationship is built on mutual respect and independence. They often say that marrying late allowed them to grow individually before growing together.

The Shift

Live for yourself first. If marriage happens, let it be a bonus—not a benchmark. You don't owe anyone a timeline. You don't need to explain your choices. You are allowed to build a life that reflects your truth—not society's expectations.

Whether you marry at 25, 45, or never—you are whole. You are worthy. You are rising.

Chapter 6
Boys Don't Cry

The Myth

"Men must be strong. Emotions are weakness."

This belief has damaged generations of men. In Indian society, boys are taught early on to suppress tears, hide vulnerability, and "man up." Crying is mocked. Sensitivity is shamed. Emotional expression is seen as feminine–and therefore, unacceptable.

The result? Men grow up emotionally stunted, unable to process grief, fear, or heartbreak. They suffer silently, often turning to anger, addiction, or isolation. Suppressing emotions doesn't make you strong–it makes you silent. And silence breeds suffering.

The Truth

Vulnerability is strength. Crying doesn't make you less of a man–it makes you human. Emotional expression is not gendered. In fact, the ability to feel deeply, express openly, and connect authentically is a sign of emotional maturity–not weakness.

Men deserve safe spaces to feel. Boys deserve to grow up knowing that their tears are valid, their fears are normal, and their softness is sacred.

Real-Life Example 1: Harsh, 28-Year-Old Teacher from Jaipur

Harsh grew up in a household where crying was punished. His father told him, "Men don't cry. Be strong." After losing a close friend in college, Harsh felt overwhelmed but couldn't bring himself to grieve openly. The bottled-up pain led to anxiety and panic attacks. It wasn't until he began therapy that he learned to express his emotions freely. Today, Harsh teaches at a boys' school and runs weekly emotional wellness circles, encouraging young boys to talk about their feelings. His journey shows that healing begins when men are allowed to feel.

Real-Life Example 2: Neeraj Ghaywan, Filmmaker

Neeraj, director of *Masaan* and *Geeli Pucchi*, has consistently portrayed emotionally complex male characters who cry, reflect, and confront their vulnerabilities. In interviews, he's spoken about how toxic masculinity limits men's emotional range and how cinema can challenge that narrative. His work has helped normalize male sensitivity in mainstream storytelling, proving that art can be a powerful tool for emotional liberation.

The Shift

Let men feel. Let boys cry. Let strength include softness. Emotional honesty is not a flaw—it's a foundation. When men are allowed to express, they become better partners, fathers, friends, and leaders.

The next generation of boys deserves to grow up knowing that tears are not weakness—they are truth.

Chapter 7
Girls Shouldn't Be Too Ambitious

The Myth

"Ambition in women is unattractive."

This belief is rooted not in tradition—but in control. In many Indian households, girls are praised for being obedient, modest, and self-sacrificing. But the moment a girl expresses bold dreams—of leading, building, or challenging norms—she's labeled "too much."

Ambition in women is often mistaken for arrogance, rebellion, or selfishness. She's told:

- "Don't aim too high—you'll intimidate others."
- "If you're too successful, men won't want to marry you."
- "Focus on family, not fame."
- "You're being aggressive, not graceful."

This conditioning doesn't just limit careers—it shrinks identities. It teaches girls to dim their light so others feel comfortable. It teaches them to apologize for wanting more.

But ambition is not aggression—it's aliveness. It's the fire that fuels change, creativity, and courage.

The Truth

Ambitious women change the world. They build companies, lead movements, write books, raise communities, and redefine what's possible.

There's nothing wrong with wanting more. There's everything right about it.

Ambition is not a betrayal of femininity—it's an expression of it. A woman's desire to rise is not a threat—it's a gift.

Real-Life Example 1: Falguni Nayar, Founder of Nykaa

Falguni Nayar left a successful career in investment banking to start Nykaa at age 50. She was told it was "too late" and "too risky." But she believed in her vision. Today, Nykaa is a billion-dollar beauty and wellness company, and Falguni is one of India's richest self-made women. Her ambition wasn't a flaw—it was her fuel.

Real-Life Example 2: Guneet Monga, Film Producer

Guneet Monga faced years of rejection in the male-dominated film industry. She didn't come from a film family. She didn't fit the mold. But she kept producing bold, meaningful stories—like *The Lunchbox* and *Period. End of Sentence*, which won an Academy Award. Her ambition didn't just build a career—it built a platform for unheard voices.

Real-Life Example 3: Richa, 26-Year-Old Civil Services Aspirant

Richa, from a small town in Bihar, was discouraged from preparing for UPSC. Her relatives said, "Girls don't need such stressful jobs." But she persisted—studying late nights, working part-time, and facing ridicule. She cleared the exam on her third attempt and now works in public administration. Her ambition wasn't arrogance–it was resilience.

The Shift

Let women rise. Let them lead. Let ambition be celebrated–not silenced.

A woman who dreams big is not a problem to be solved–she's a force to be respected. Her ambition is not a threat to tradition–it's a bridge to transformation.

If you're a woman with bold dreams, don't shrink to fit. Don't wait for permission. Don't trade your fire for approval.

You're not too much. You're just enough to change everything.

Chapter 8
Follow the Timeline

The Myth

"By 25, be settled. By 30, be married. By 35, be successful."

This timeline is drilled into young minds across India. It's not written anywhere officially, but it's everywhere–spoken in family gatherings, implied in job interviews, echoed in wedding invitations. It's the invisible checklist that defines what a "normal" life should look like.

If you deviate from it, the questions begin:

- "Still studying? At this age?"
- "Not married yet? What are you waiting for?"
- "Changing careers now? Isn't it too late?"
- "You're still figuring things out? You should be settled by now."

This timeline doesn't account for personal growth, mental health, financial realities, or individual dreams. It assumes everyone starts from the same place and moves at the same pace. But life isn't a conveyor belt–it's a canvas. And timelines, when imposed, become traps.

The Truth

You're not late. You're not early. You're right on time–for your own story.

Growth doesn't follow a clock. Some people find their calling at 16, others at 60. Some marry young and thrive. Others marry late–or never–and still live deeply fulfilling lives. The idea that success, love, or stability must arrive by a certain age is not just false–it's harmful.

Comparison kills joy. Timelines kill truth. Your journey is valid, even if it doesn't look like anyone else's.

Real-Life Example 1: Colonel Harland Sanders

Colonel Sanders founded KFC at the age of 65. Before that, he held dozens of jobs–from steam engine stoker to insurance salesman. He faced rejection, bankruptcy, and ridicule. But he didn't give up. His story proves that success doesn't expire–it evolves.

Real-Life Example 2: Julia Child

Julia Child published her first cookbook at 50 and became a world-renowned chef and television personality in her 60s. She didn't grow up cooking. She didn't follow a traditional path. But her passion led her to a legacy that outlived every timeline.

Real-Life Example 3: Amitabh Bachchan

After a slump in his career during the 1990s, Amitabh Bachchan reinvented himself in his 60s with roles that showcased depth, vulnerability, and gravitas. From *Kaun Banega Crorepati* to *Black* and *Piku*, he proved that resurgence is always possible–and that age can be an asset, not a limitation.

Real-Life Example 4: Radhika, 38-Year-Old Designer from Delhi

Radhika spent her twenties in a corporate job she didn't love. At 35, she quit to study textile design. Friends called her "impulsive." Relatives said she was "too old to start over." Today, she runs a boutique that ships globally and mentors young designers. Her timeline didn't match the norm—but it matched her truth.

The Shift

Live at your own pace. Your rise is yours alone.

There is no deadline for becoming who you're meant to be. Whether you bloom early or late, whether you take detours or pause to heal—your path is valid. The only timeline that matters is the one that honors your growth, your values, and your joy.

Chapter 9
"Don't Talk About Mental Health"

The Myth

"Mental health issues are shameful. Keep it private. Be strong."

This myth is deeply rooted in Indian society, where emotional struggles are often dismissed as weakness or drama. People are told to "move on," "pray more," or "stay busy," as if mental illness is a phase or a choice. The silence around mental health has created generations of people suffering quietly, afraid to seek help.

The Truth

Mental health is just as real as physical health. Depression, anxiety, trauma, and burnout are not signs of weakness–they're signs that something needs attention. Talking about it isn't shameful–it's healing. Seeking therapy isn't indulgent–it's survival.

Example 1: Deepika Padukone

One of India's most celebrated actresses, Deepika publicly shared her battle with depression in 2015. At the peak of her career, she felt empty and hopeless. Instead of hiding it, she spoke out, started therapy, and launched the **Live Love Laugh Foundation** to support mental health awareness. Her courage helped normalize therapy and inspired thousands to seek help.

Example 2: Rohan Verma, Student & Podcaster

Rohan, a 21-year-old engineering student from Pune, suffered severe anxiety during his final year. Panic attacks, sleepless nights, and isolation became routine. After months of silence, he began therapy and started a podcast called *Mind Over Matter*, where he shares his journey and interviews psychologists. His platform now reaches over 50,000 listeners, helping young Indians feel seen and supported.

The Shift

Mental health needs to be part of everyday conversation–in homes, schools, workplaces. You don't have to suffer in silence. You don't have to pretend. Healing begins when you speak. Strength begins when you seek help.

Chapter 10
"Success Means a Government Job"

The Myth

"A secure government job is the only real success. Everything else is risky."

This belief is especially strong in middle-class Indian families. Government jobs are seen as the gold standard–stable income, pension, social respect. But this mindset often ignores passion, creativity, and the evolving job market. It also dismisses entrepreneurship and innovation as "unstable" or "unrealistic."

The Truth

Success isn't defined by job security–it's defined by **fulfillment, impact, and growth**. Government jobs are noble, but they're not the only path. Today's world offers countless opportunities in startups, tech, media, and social enterprise. Choosing your own path isn't risky–it's revolutionary.

Example 1: Kunal Shah, Entrepreneur

Kunal left a well-paying job to start **FreeCharge**, a mobile payments platform. After its success, he launched **CRED**, which became one of India's most talked-about fintech startups. He didn't follow the government job route–he created jobs. His story proves that innovation can be just as impactful as tradition.

Example 2: Priya Sharma, UPSC Aspirant Turned Creator

Priya spent five years preparing for the civil services exam. After multiple failed attempts, she pivoted to content creation, sharing study tips and motivational videos. Her YouTube channel now has over 1 million subscribers, and she earns more than most bureaucrats. She turned disappointment into a digital empire.

The Shift

Success is personal. It's not about titles–it's about purpose. Whether you're a civil servant or a startup founder, what matters is that you chose your path–not someone else's.

Chapter 11
"Art Isn't a Real Career"

The Myth

"Art is a hobby, not a profession. It won't feed you."

This belief is deeply rooted in Indian households. Whether it's painting, music, poetry, theatre, or comedy–art is often dismissed as a side interest, something to be pursued only after securing a 'real' job. Parents discourage it, schools underfund it, and society undervalues it.

Young people with creative talent are told:

- "You'll end up broke."
- "No one respects artists."
- "Do it for fun, not for a living."
- "What will people say if you don't become an engineer or IAS officer?"

This mindset has crushed countless dreams. It has forced painters into cubicles, poets into code, and musicians into silence. But the truth is: art is not just real–it's revolutionary.

The Truth

Art is a career. A powerful one. It builds culture, challenges norms, heals wounds, and moves hearts. Artists are not escapists–they are architects of emotion, memory, and meaning.

A career in art demands discipline, resilience, and vision. It may not follow a fixed path, but it offers something rare: freedom, expression, and impact. And yes—it can pay the bills, build empires, and change lives.

Real-Life Example 1: Kapil Sharma, Comedian and Actor

Kapil Sharma came from a modest background in Amritsar. He didn't have industry connections or financial backing. But he had timing, wit, and relentless drive. Despite being mocked for choosing comedy over a "serious" profession, he won *The Great Indian Laughter Challenge*, built *Comedy Nights with Kapil*, and became one of India's highest-paid entertainers. His journey proves that humor is not just art—it's enterprise.

Real-Life Example 2: Zakir Khan, Poet and Stand-Up Artist

Zakir Khan was told he wasn't "hero material." He didn't fit the mold—no fancy accent, no polished persona. But he had stories. He blended poetry, vulnerability, and humor to create a style that resonated with millions. His rise from rejection to sold-out shows and viral specials is a testament to the power of authenticity. Zakir didn't just build a career—he built a movement for middle-class expression.

Real-Life Example 3: Rukmini Devi Arundale, Bharatanatyam Pioneer

In the early 20th century, Bharatanatyam was stigmatized and dismissed. Rukmini Devi, born into an elite Brahmin family, chose to revive and elevate it. She founded Kalakshetra, a premier arts academy, and redefined classical dance as a respected profession. Her legacy lives on in every stage that honors Indian tradition.

The Shift

Art is not a detour–it's a destination. You don't need to apologize for choosing creativity. You don't need to justify your passion. Whether you're a dancer, filmmaker, cartoonist, or storyteller–your work matters.

Chapter 12
"You Must Always Avoid Conflict to Be Good"

The Myth

"Good people don't fight. Avoid conflict at all costs."

In many families, especially for women, avoiding confrontation is seen as a virtue. You're taught to "adjust," "let it go," or "keep quiet" to maintain harmony. But **avoiding conflict often means avoiding truth.** It allows injustice, manipulation, and disrespect to thrive.

The Truth

Conflict isn't bad–it's necessary. Standing up for yourself doesn't make you difficult–it makes you clear. Growth often begins with uncomfortable conversations.

Example 1: Medha Patkar, social activist

Medha led the Narmada Bachao Andolan, challenging powerful institutions and government policies. Her activism involved constant conflict–but it protected thousands of displaced families. Her courage proved that fighting for justice is a form of goodness.

Example 2: Ravi, a young employee in Noida

Ravi's manager repeatedly gave him credit for team work but denied him promotions. After months of silence, Ravi confronted the issue professionally and escalated it to HR. The result: a promotion, a pay raise, and a shift in team dynamics. His conflict led to clarity.

The Shift

Avoiding conflict doesn't make you noble–it makes you invisible. **Speak. Stand. Rise.**

Chapter 13
"You Must Always Be the Same Person Everywhere"

The Myth

"Don't change. Be consistent. People won't trust you if you evolve too much."

In our society, especially in tight-knit communities, changing your opinions, style, or ambitions is often seen as "confusion" or "fakeness." You're expected to pick one identity and stick to it. But **growth demands transformation.** You're not meant to stay the same–you're meant to evolve.

The Truth

You're allowed to change. You can be spiritual and ambitious, introverted and outspoken, traditional and progressive. You're a mosaic–not a label.

Example 1: Masaba Gupta, fashion designer

Masaba started as a designer known for bold prints and unconventional styles. Later, she became an actor, entrepreneur, and mental health advocate. Her evolution wasn't inconsistency–it was expansion.

Example 2: Ravi, a former banker turned yoga teacher

Ravi left his high-paying job to pursue wellness. His friends mocked him for "changing too much." Today, he runs a successful yoga retreat and teaches financial literacy to wellness professionals. His journey proves that reinvention is strength.

The Shift

You don't owe anyone a fixed version of yourself. You're allowed to grow, shift, and rise—again and again.

Chapter 14
"Siblings Must Always Sacrifice for Each Other"

The Myth

"Good siblings always adjust. You must sacrifice for your brother or sister–no matter what."

In many Indian families, sibling relationships are idealized as lifelong bonds of duty and sacrifice. While love and support between siblings can be beautiful, this myth often turns into emotional pressure. One sibling is expected to give up opportunities, stay silent during conflict, or carry the burden of family expectations–all in the name of "being good."

Common phrases include:

- "Let your brother go first–you'll get your chance later."
- "She's younger–adjust for her."
- "Don't fight. You're siblings–you must always stay united."
- "If you succeed, make sure your sibling doesn't feel left behind."

This belief can lead to resentment, suppressed dreams, and unequal treatment. It teaches people to prioritize harmony over honesty, and sacrifice over self-respect.

The Truth

Support between siblings should be mutual—not one-sided. You are allowed to have boundaries, ambitions, and disagreements. You are not selfish for choosing your own path. You are not disloyal for speaking up.

Healthy sibling relationships are built on respect—not obligation. You can love your sibling and still say no. You can care deeply and still choose differently.

Real-Life Example 1: Ananya, 24-Year-Old Engineer

Ananya was offered a scholarship to study abroad, but her parents asked her to decline so her younger brother could have a chance first. She struggled with guilt but eventually chose to go. Her brother later thanked her for showing him what courage looks like. Today, both siblings are thriving—because she chose growth over guilt.

Real-Life Example 2: Arjun and Meera, Siblings from Pune

Meera always felt overshadowed by Arjun, who was the "golden child." She was expected to support him emotionally, academically, and even financially. After years of silent resentment, she confronted her family and asked for equal recognition. It was uncomfortable—but transformative. Today, Meera runs her own business and shares a healthier, more honest bond with her brother.

The Shift

You don't owe your sibling your silence. You don't owe them your future. You owe them honesty, respect, and love—but not self-erasure.

Let siblinghood be a space for growth, not guilt. Let it be a bond—not a burden.

Chapter 15
Going Abroad Means You've Abandoned Your Country

The Myth

"If you leave India to study or earn, you're not patriotic. You've given up on your roots."

This belief is quietly embedded in many Indian families and communities. Going abroad is often seen as turning your back on your homeland–as if ambition and migration are acts of betrayal. The assumption is that if you truly loved your country, you'd stay and "fix the system" from within.

People who choose to leave are told:

- "You're running away."
- "You've forgotten your culture."
- "You should stay and serve your nation."
- "Life is hard here–but that's what makes it meaningful."

This mindset romanticizes struggle and guilt-trips ambition. It assumes that staying in a broken system is more noble than seeking growth elsewhere. But life is too short to fight every battle just to prove loyalty. And patriotism isn't about suffering–it's about contribution.

The Truth

Leaving your country doesn't mean leaving your values. You can love your homeland and still choose a different path. You can carry your culture wherever you go. You can contribute to India from anywhere in the world–through ideas, innovation, investment, or inspiration.

Patriotism isn't about geography–it's about integrity. It's not about staying–it's about serving, in whatever way you're best equipped to.

Real-Life Example 1: Satya Nadella, CEO of Microsoft

Born and raised in Hyderabad, Satya Nadella moved to the U.S. for higher education and built a career in technology. Today, he leads one of the world's largest companies and actively supports Indian innovation, education, and entrepreneurship. Under his leadership, Microsoft has invested heavily in India's digital infrastructure, cloud services, and AI research. He's also spoken about the importance of inclusive growth and empowering Indian youth through technology.

Real-Life Example 2: Roshni, 29-Year-Old Researcher in Germany

Roshni left India to pursue a PhD in climate science. Her relatives accused her of "giving up" on India's problems. But her research now helps South Asian governments prepare for climate disasters. She collaborates with Indian NGOs and mentors students back home. Her impact is borderless–and deeply patriotic.

Real-Life Example 3: Priyanka Chopra Jonas, Actor and Producer

Priyanka built her career in Bollywood, then expanded globally. She's faced criticism for "leaving India behind." Yet she continues to produce Indian stories, support Indian causes, and represent Indian identity on global platforms. Her success abroad has opened doors for countless others.

Real-Life Example 4: Karan Aujla, Punjabi Singer and Lyricist

Born in Ghurala village, Ludhiana, Karan Aujla lost both parents at a young age and moved to Canada as a teenager. While working part-time jobs and studying, he nurtured his passion for music. Today, he's one of the most influential Punjabi artists globally. His lyrics reflect the pride, pain, and resilience of Indian identity. He's tattooed the faces of Bhagat Singh and Udham Singh on his body–a visible reminder that distance doesn't erase belonging. Karan didn't abandon India. He amplified it. His success abroad gave Punjabi music a global stage, proving that cultural pride and international ambition can coexist.

The Shift

You don't owe anyone a fixed location. You owe yourself growth, freedom, and truth.

Let go of the guilt. Let go of the pressure to stay and suffer just to prove your love. You can rise anywhere–and still carry your country with you.

Patriotism isn't about staying stuck. It's about rising–and lifting others as you do.

Part Ten

The Inner Mechanics of Change

Chapter 1
The Habit Loop — How Repetition Shapes Identity

Habits are the brain's way of conserving energy. In evolutionary terms, they allowed early humans to perform essential tasks–like gathering food or building shelter–without constant decision-making. Neuroscientist Ann Graybiel discovered that habits are encoded in the basal ganglia, a part of the brain responsible for automatic behavior. Once a habit is formed, it runs on a loop: cue, routine, reward. The brain stops participating in the decision and simply executes. This automation is powerful–but also dangerous. Habits can be life-giving or life-limiting.

To understand how habits shape us, we must explore three key psychological principles. First, neuroplasticity–the brain's ability to rewire itself through repeated experience. Every time we repeat a behavior, we strengthen the neural pathways that support it. This is how habits become automatic, and how addiction hijacks the brain's reward system. But neuroplasticity also offers hope: with consistent effort, we can carve new paths and reshape our emotional landscape.

Second, temporal discounting–the tendency to prioritize short-term rewards over long-term benefits. This bias explains why we procrastinate, overeat, or relapse into old patterns. The future feels distant, while the present feels urgent. Healing requires emotional anchoring: making the future feel real enough to influence today's choices. When we connect our actions to a deeper identity or vision, we begin to override the impulse for instant gratification.

Third, implementation intentions–mental scripts that link specific cues to specific actions. Psychologist Peter Gollwitzer found that people who use "If–Then" plans are far more likely to follow through on goals. For example: "If I feel anxious at night, then I'll take a cold shower and journal." These scripts reduce decision fatigue and create readiness. They turn vague intentions into concrete behaviors, helping the brain respond automatically in moments of vulnerability.

Real-life example: Jason, a recovering heroin addict from Ohio, began using at 17 to escape childhood trauma. What started as occasional use became daily dependence. After multiple relapses, he entered a rehab program that focused on habit replacement–substituting drug use with journaling, group therapy, and fitness. Each new behavior activated neuroplasticity, slowly rewiring his brain. "I had to rebuild my identity," he says. "Not just quit the drug."

Similarly, Arjun, a college student in Pune, struggled with compulsive masturbation tied to anxiety and isolation. The short-term relief always won, a classic case of temporal discounting. Through therapy, he learned to visualize his future self–calm, connected, and confident. That image helped him choose meditation over impulse. He also used implementation intentions like "If I feel lonely at night, then I'll call a friend or go for a walk." These tiny plans became anchors. They didn't just change his behavior–they changed his relationship with himself.

Healing from destructive habits requires compassion, structure, and support. Tools like habit tracking, environmental design, and identity-based goals help reshape behavior. Instead of saying "I want to quit," we say "This isn't who I want to be anymore–and I'm ready to show up differently." The brain follows identity. When we change the story, we change the loop. Habits aren't cages–they're keys. And with the right guidance, even the most deeply ingrained patterns can be rewritten into a life of purpose and peace.

Chapter 2
The Postponement Trap — Why We Delay What Matters

Postponement is often mistaken for laziness, but it's usually fear in disguise. We delay tasks that feel emotionally risky—writing that vulnerable email, starting a creative project, or making a life change. Psychologist Tim Pychyl found that procrastination is not a time-management issue, but an emotion-regulation problem. We avoid discomfort, not deadlines. The brain seeks short-term relief, even at long-term cost.

Evolutionarily, postponement had survival value. In uncertain environments, delaying action allowed time for more information or safer conditions. But in modern life, this instinct can sabotage growth. A 2023 study in Nature Human Behaviour showed that chronic procrastinators have higher levels of stress, lower well-being, and even poorer physical health. The delay becomes a drain.

Real-life example: Omar, a musician in Cairo, postponed releasing his album for three years. He feared criticism and failure. A coach helped him break the project into micro-tasks—one song, one mix, one upload. He released it in stages and received overwhelming support. "I realized I was postponing joy," he says. "Not just work." His fear didn't vanish, but his courage grew louder.

Coping with postponement means shifting focus from perfection to progress. Tools like the Pomodoro technique, emotional journaling, and accountability partners help bridge the gap between intention and action. When we stop waiting for the perfect moment, we start living in the real one. Postponement isn't a flaw—it's a signal. And when we listen, we move.

Chapter 3
The Spotlight Effect — You're Not Being Watched

The spotlight effect is a psychological illusion that convinces us we're constantly being observed, judged, or evaluated by others. Psychologists Thomas Gilovich and Kenneth Savitsky coined the term after a series of experiments revealed that people consistently overestimate how much attention others pay to their appearance, mistakes, or behavior. This distortion fuels social anxiety and self-consciousness, making us feel like we're on stage even when no one is watching. The truth is, most people are too absorbed in their own thoughts to scrutinize ours.

This illusion is rooted in egocentrism—not arrogance, but the natural tendency to anchor perception in our own experience. Evolutionarily, being noticed by the tribe could mean survival or danger, so the brain developed a hyper-awareness of social cues. But in modern life, this instinct often misfires. A stain on our shirt, a mispronounced word, or a moment of awkwardness feels catastrophic, when in reality, it barely registers in others' minds. Studies published in Personality and Social Psychology Bulletin show that people remember their own social blunders far more vividly than others do.

Real-life example: Nina, a dancer in New York, feared wearing bold outfits. She believed everyone was watching, silently judging her choices. Her coach challenged her to wear red lipstick for a week—

something she'd always wanted to try but avoided. No one commented. No one stared. "I realized people are too busy living their own lives," she said. That experiment became a turning point. She began dressing for herself, not for approval. Her confidence grew not because others changed—but because her perception did.

Coping with the spotlight effect begins with reframing. Instead of assuming others are watching, we remind ourselves that they're likely navigating their own insecurities. Exposure therapy—intentionally doing things that trigger self-consciousness—can help desensitize the fear. Journaling, mindfulness, and self-compassion practices also help shift focus inward, toward authenticity rather than performance. The goal isn't to be invisible—it's to be unapologetically visible without needing permission. When we stop performing and start living, the spotlight fades—and the light within us begins to shine.

Chapter 4
The Loneliness Paradox — Alone in a Connected World

Loneliness isn't just the absence of people–it's the absence of connection. In today's hyperconnected world, we can message someone across the globe in seconds, yet still feel emotionally isolated. This paradox has become one of the defining psychological challenges of our time. A 2020 study by Cigna revealed that over 60% of Americans regularly feel lonely, despite being surrounded by digital networks. Neuroscientist John Cacioppo found that loneliness activates the same brain regions as physical pain, suggesting that emotional disconnection is not just sad–it's biologically distressing.

From an evolutionary perspective, loneliness was a survival alarm. In tribal societies, isolation meant vulnerability to predators and starvation. The brain evolved to interpret social exclusion as a threat, triggering stress responses to motivate reconnection. But in modern life, this alarm often misfires. We scroll through curated lives, compare ourselves to filtered perfection, and mistake visibility for intimacy. The more we perform connection, the less we feel it. Loneliness becomes a quiet ache beneath the noise.

Real-life example: Alex, a graphic designer in Berlin, had thousands of followers and a thriving online presence. Yet he felt emotionally hollow. Likes didn't translate to love. He joined a local book club and began attending therapy. Sharing vulnerably helped him build real relationships. “I stopped performing and started showing up,” he says. His healing didn’t come from more people–it came from deeper presence. The shift wasn’t external–it was emotional.

Chapter 5
Cognitive Distortions — The Mind's Funhouse Mirror

The human mind is a master storyteller–but not always a truthful one. Cognitive distortions are biased patterns of thinking that warp reality, often amplifying fear, shame, or self-doubt. Psychologist Aaron Beck first identified these distortions while treating depression, noticing that patients consistently misinterpreted neutral events as negative. These mental filters act like a funhouse mirror, exaggerating flaws and minimizing strengths. We begin to believe thoughts like "I'm a failure" or "No one cares," not because they're true, but because they've been repeated.

Common distortions include catastrophizing (expecting the worst), personalization (blaming ourselves for everything), and black-and-white thinking (seeing things as all good or all bad). These patterns often form in childhood, shaped by trauma, criticism, or unstable environments. Over time, they become automatic. The brain, trying to protect us, creates shortcuts–but these shortcuts can lead us into emotional dead ends. A 2021 meta-analysis in Clinical Psychology Review confirmed that cognitive distortions are strongly linked to anxiety, depression, and low self-esteem across cultures.

Real-life example: Priya, a university student in Mumbai, failed one exam and immediately concluded she was unworthy of her degree. Her therapist helped her identify "all-or-nothing" thinking and challenged her to find evidence for and against that belief. Through journaling and CBT exercises, Priya began to reframe her thoughts: "One test doesn't define me. I've succeeded before, and I can again." Her anxiety didn't vanish overnight, but her relationship with her mind began to shift. She started seeing thoughts as suggestions—not facts.

Chapter 6
The Hedonic Treadmill — Why Happiness Keeps Moving

We chase happiness like a finish line, believing that once we reach a goal–be it a promotion, a relationship, or a dream home–we'll finally feel fulfilled. But the brain adapts quickly. This phenomenon, known as the hedonic treadmill, reveals that after a burst of joy, we return to our emotional baseline. Psychologists Brickman and Campbell coined the term in 1971, and studies since then have confirmed that even major life events–winning the lottery or surviving trauma–don't permanently alter our happiness levels.

This adaptation is both a blessing and a trap. It protects us from prolonged suffering but also dulls the joy of achievement. A 2024 study published in Springer modeled hedonic cycles using the approach-avoidance framework, showing how people oscillate between pleasure and dissatisfaction, driven by shifting desires. The treadmill keeps moving, and we keep running–chasing the next high, the next validation, the next "finally."

Real-life example: Sarah, a tech entrepreneur from San Francisco, sold her startup for millions. She expected euphoria, but instead felt empty. Therapy helped her realize she'd tied her worth to achievement. She began practicing gratitude journaling and volunteering weekly–activities that brought sustained joy. The treadmill slowed when she stopped running toward happiness and started walking with it.

Chapter 7
The Arrival Fallacy — "I'll Be Happy When..."

The arrival fallacy convinces us that happiness lies just beyond the next milestone. Harvard psychologist Tal Ben-Shahar coined this term to describe the emotional letdown after success. Dopamine spikes during pursuit, but drops after attainment, leaving us disoriented. We expect joy to arrive with achievement, but often feel underwhelmed. This fallacy is reinforced by societal narratives that equate success with happiness.

We postpone joy, believing it must be earned. But the truth is, fulfillment doesn't come from arrival–it comes from alignment. A study from the University of Pennsylvania found that people who focus on intrinsic goals–growth, connection, contribution–report higher well-being than those chasing external rewards. The fallacy keeps us emotionally suspended, always waiting for life to begin.

Real-life example: Rohan, a civil service aspirant in Delhi, spent five years preparing for the UPSC exam. When he finally cleared it, he expected peace. Instead, anxiety crept in about performance and expectations. Through mindfulness and therapy, he learned to find joy in daily rituals–morning walks, cooking, and connecting with friends. Fulfillment wasn't in the title; it was in the texture of life.

Chapter 8
Learned Helplessness — When Depression Teaches Us to Stop Trying

When repeated setbacks convince us that effort is futile, the brain enters a state called learned helplessness. Martin Seligman's experiments in the 1960s showed that animals exposed to uncontrollable pain stopped trying to escape–even when escape was possible. In humans, this manifests as depression, where hopelessness becomes a default state. It's not laziness–it's a survival adaptation gone awry.

This psychological paralysis is reinforced by failure, trauma, and invalidation. The brain learns that action leads to pain, so it stops acting. A 2023 study in Nature Mental Health found that learned helplessness is linked to reduced activity in the prefrontal cortex–the part responsible for decision-making and motivation. The longer we stay stuck, the harder it becomes to believe in change.

Real-life example: James, a veteran in Texas, struggled with PTSD and unemployment. After years of rejection, he stopped applying for jobs. A support group introduced him to micro-goals–sending one email a day, walking for ten minutes. Slowly, his confidence returned. He now mentors others through the VA. Healing wasn't a leap–it was a series of steps toward agency.

Chapter 9
The Sunk Cost Fallacy — Why We Stay Too Long

The sunk cost fallacy is the tendency to continue investing in something–relationships, careers, habits–simply because we've already invested time, money, or energy. Psychologist Hal Arkes found that people often make irrational decisions to avoid feeling wasteful. But staying in the wrong place doesn't reclaim the past–it sacrifices the future. The fallacy traps us in cycles of regret and resistance.

Evolutionarily, commitment was tied to survival. Abandoning a hunt or a shelter too soon could mean death. But in modern life, this instinct misfires. We stay in draining jobs, toxic relationships, or outdated dreams, fearing that leaving means failure. A 2023 study in Behavioral Economics Journal showed that people who let go of sunk costs reported higher life satisfaction and emotional clarity.

Real-life example: Ayaan, a software engineer in Dubai, spent six years building a startup that never took off. He kept pushing, fearing that quitting would make the years feel wasted. A mentor helped him reframe: "You didn't fail–you learned." He closed the company and joined a nonprofit, finding purpose and peace. "Letting go gave me back my life," he says.

Coping with the sunk cost fallacy means honoring what we've learned, not what we've lost. Reflection, reframing, and future-focused decision-making help us move forward. The past is a teacher, not a trap. When we stop trying to justify the investment and start choosing alignment, we rise—not because we held on, but because we knew when to release.

Chapter 10
Emotional Contagion — How Feelings Spread Like Fire

Emotions are social signals. We don't just feel them–we catch them. This phenomenon, known as emotional contagion, was first studied by psychologist Elaine Hatfield. It refers to the unconscious transmission of mood and affect between people. When someone near us is anxious, joyful, or angry, our brain mirrors their state through neural mechanisms like mirror neurons. We absorb their energy, often without realizing it.

This principle explains why environments matter. A toxic workplace, a tense household, or a chaotic social feed can shape our emotional landscape. A 2023 study in Psychological Science found that people exposed to negative emotional expressions–even briefly–showed increased cortisol levels and reduced cognitive performance. Emotional contagion isn't just psychological–it's physiological. We don't just hear emotions–we embody them.

Real-life example: Rishi, a customer service rep in Bengaluru, noticed that his mood dipped after every shift. His team was constantly stressed, sarcastic, and reactive. He began wearing noise-canceling headphones during breaks, listening to calming music, and practicing breathwork before meetings. "I couldn't change the room," he says. "But I could change my response." Over time, his resilience grew, and he became a source of calm for others.

Part Eleven

The Divinity

Chapter 1
Stillness Speaks

Stillness isn't emptiness–it's presence. It's where clarity lives and the soul whispers.

In a world that glorifies noise, speed, and constant movement, stillness is often misunderstood. It's seen as laziness, passivity, or emptiness. But stillness is not the absence of action–it's the presence of awareness. It's where clarity lives. It's where the mind exhales and the soul listens.

Stillness isn't a luxury–it's a necessity. It's where healing begins, where wisdom grows, and where transformation takes root. In the quiet, you don't lose yourself–you find yourself. Let stillness speak. It has been waiting patiently for you to listen.

Real-Life Examples

- *Anaya*, 34, began meditating for five minutes a day. She found that silence didn't just calm her–it revealed her.
- Anika, 29 – The Break That Brought Her BackAnika was always busy–meetings, deadlines, social events. She felt productive but perpetually exhausted. One weekend, she canceled everything and sat in silence. No phone, no plans. Just stillness. At first, it felt uncomfortable. Then, it felt like coming home.

In that quiet, she realized she'd been ignoring her own needs. She journaled, cried, and slept deeply. That pause didn't derail her–it realigned her. Stillness gave her the clarity to make changes she'd been avoiding.

- Rohan, 42 – The Power of a Silent WalkRohan was facing a major life decision: whether to leave a secure job for a passion project. Advice poured in from all sides, but his mind felt cluttered. One evening, he went for a walk–no music, no calls, just footsteps and air.

In that silence, the noise settled. His thoughts became clearer. He didn't find a perfect answer, but he found peace with the uncertainty. That walk didn't solve everything–but it helped him trust himself again.

- Meera, 35 – Meditation as a MirrorMeera started meditating not to become "spiritual," but to manage anxiety. At first, she hated it–her mind raced, her body fidgeted. But over time, she noticed something: the stillness didn't silence her thoughts–it helped her see them.

She began recognizing patterns, triggers, and stories she'd been telling herself. Stillness became her mirror. It didn't erase her struggles–it helped her understand them.

"The soul is neither born, and nor does it die." – *Bhagavad Gita 2.20*
"The quieter you become, the more you can hear." – *Ram Dass*

Principle to Rise: Inner Listening Stillness is not passive–it's powerful. Let it speak.

Chapter 2
Faith in the Unseen

Spirituality is trusting what you can't yet prove. It's believing in the invisible threads that hold life together.

Faith in the unseen is the quiet force that moves us forward when logic says stop. It's the belief that something better is coming, even when there's no proof. It's not blind optimism—it's inner knowing. The kind that whispers, "*Keep going,*" when the world says, "*Give up.*"

In a society obsessed with evidence and guarantees, faith is often dismissed. But some of the most powerful transformations begin in uncertainty. Faith isn't about having all the answers—it's about trusting the process, the timing, and yourself.

Real-Life Examples

- **Aarzoo, 26 – The Leap Without a Net** Aarzoo left her corporate job to pursue her dream of becoming a full-time artist. She had no clients, no savings cushion, and no roadmap. Friends called her reckless. But something inside her said, "*This is the right path.*"

For months, she faced rejection and doubt. But she kept painting, kept posting, kept believing. A year later, her work was featured in a national gallery. Her success didn't come from certainty—it came from faith in the unseen.

- **Pranav, 39 – Healing Without Guarantees** After a difficult divorce, Pranav felt broken. Therapy helped, but progress was slow. He couldn't see the light at the end of the tunnel. Still, he showed up–week after week–trusting that healing would come.

One day, he realized he hadn't cried in months. He was laughing more, sleeping better, reconnecting with friends. The shift was gradual, invisible at first. But his faith in the process led him to peace he never thought possible.

- **Ishita, 33 – The Startup That Almost Didn't Start** Ishita had an idea for a wellness app but no funding, no team, and no tech background. She pitched it anyway. Investors passed. Developers ghosted. But she kept refining her vision, trusting that the right people would find her.

Eventually, a small accelerator took her in. Her app launched six months later and gained traction. Ishita's journey wasn't built on certainty–it was built on belief. She saw something no one else did–and held onto it until it became real.

- **Zayan, 41 – The Faith to Forgive** Zayan's brother betrayed him in a business deal. The fallout was painful and public. Everyone told him to cut ties. But Zayan chose forgiveness–not because it was easy, but because he believed in healing beyond revenge.

Years later, his brother returned with an apology and a changed heart. Their relationship didn't just recover–it deepened. Zayan's faith in reconciliation gave both of them a second chance.

"Faith is taking the first step even when you don't see the whole staircase." – *Martin Luther King Jr.*

Principle to Rise: Trustful Surrender: Let go of control. Lean into trust.

Chapter 3
The Divine in Daily Life

We often imagine the divine as distant–locked in temples, scriptures, or rituals. But what if it's closer than we think? What if the sacred lives in the mundane: a shared smile, a quiet sunrise, a moment of kindness? The divine isn't always dramatic. Sometimes, it's subtle. It shows up in the rhythm of everyday life, asking not for worship, but for awareness. It's in your morning tea, your child's laughter, your breath.

To see the divine in daily life is to shift from seeking miracles to noticing them. It's not about religion–it's about reverence. It's about slowing down enough to feel the presence of something greater in the smallest things.

Real-Life Examples

- **Aanya, 34 – The Prayer in a Cup of Tea** Every morning, Aanya made tea for her aging father. It was a simple ritual–boil water, add leaves, pour gently. But over time, she realized this act was more than routine. It was devotion. It was love in motion.

One day, her father said, "*Your tea tastes like peace.*" That moment stayed with her. She understood that the divine wasn't just in temples–it was in her kitchen, in her care, in her presence.

- **Raghav, 40 – The Sacredness of Silence** Raghav used to fill every moment with noise–podcasts, news, calls. But after a personal loss, he began sitting quietly on his balcony each evening. No agenda. Just stillness.

In that silence, he began to feel something deeper–a connection to nature, to memory, to spirit. The breeze felt like a blessing. The stars felt like witnesses. He didn't find God in words–he found it in quiet.

- **Meher, 28 – The Divine in Service** Meher volunteered at a local shelter once a week. She didn't see herself as spiritual–just someone trying to help. But one evening, a child hugged her and whispered, *"You're like magic."*

That moment cracked something open. She realized that compassion is divine. That showing up for others is sacred. She didn't need a sermon–she needed presence.

- **Zubin, 36 – The Blessing of Breath** After recovering from a serious illness, Zubin began practicing mindful breathing. At first, it was just a health habit. But soon, each inhale felt like grace. Each exhale felt like release.

He began to see his body as a temple–not perfect, but holy. The divine wasn't outside him–it was within. Every breath became a prayer.

Quotes

"When you do things from your soul, you feel a river moving in you, a joy." – *Rumi*

Principle to Rise: Sacred Presence: Every moment is holy—if you choose to see it that way.

Chapter 4
Letting Go to Grow

Growth isn't just about adding–it's about releasing. Letting go is one of the most transformative acts we can choose. It means shedding old beliefs, toxic relationships, outdated goals, and emotional baggage that weigh us down. It's not easy. It often feels like loss. But in truth, it's space-making–for clarity, peace, and new beginnings.

We hold on because we're afraid: afraid of change, of emptiness, of regret. But holding on to what hurts only delays healing. Letting go isn't weakness–it's wisdom. It's trusting that what's ahead is worth more than what's behind.

Real-Life Examples

- Aarav, 38 – Letting Go of a Career That No Longer Fit Aarav had worked in finance for over a decade. It paid well, but he felt disconnected. He dreamed of teaching but feared judgment and financial instability. Still, the inner pull grew stronger.

Eventually, he left his job and began tutoring part-time. The transition was slow, but his joy returned. Letting go of prestige gave him purpose. He didn't lose status–he found meaning.

- Sana, 27 – Releasing a Friendship That Had Expired Sana had a childhood friend who constantly criticized her choices and dismissed her growth. Every conversation left her drained. She held on out of loyalty and nostalgia.

After a particularly hurtful exchange, Sana chose silence. She didn't confront—she simply stopped chasing connection that no longer felt safe. In that space, new friendships blossomed. Letting go wasn't cruel—it was self-care.

- Kabir, 42 – Letting Go of Resentment Kabir had been hurt by a family member years ago. Though they had apologized, he held onto the pain. It became part of his identity—bitterness disguised as protection.

Through therapy and reflection, Kabir realized that forgiveness wasn't about forgetting—it was about freeing himself. He let go of the story that kept him stuck. The moment he released resentment, peace entered.

"Some of us think holding on makes us strong, but sometimes it is letting go." – *Hermann Hesse*

Principle to Rise: Sacred Release: Let go—not to lose, but to lighten.

Chapter 5
Nature as Teacher

Nature doesn't speak in words—but it teaches with every sunrise, every storm, every cycle. It reminds us that growth takes time, that seasons change, and that stillness is just as important as movement. When we slow down and observe, we realize that nature isn't just scenery—it's wisdom in motion.

From the resilience of trees to the patience of rivers, nature models the qualities we often forget in our fast-paced lives. It doesn't rush. It doesn't force. It simply unfolds. And in doing so, it invites us to do the same.

Real-Life Examples

- **Aadil, 39 – Learning Resilience from a Banyan Tree** After losing his job unexpectedly, Aadil felt uprooted and defeated. One afternoon, he sat under a massive banyan tree near his home. He noticed how its roots stretched wide, anchoring it through storms and seasons.

That tree had stood for decades—weathering change, growing slowly but surely. Aadil began journaling under it weekly, drawing strength from its quiet endurance. Nature didn't fix his problems—but it reminded him that stability comes from deep roots, not fast growth.

- **Charvi, 28 – Finding Flow in the River** Charvi was overwhelmed by decisions–career, relationships, identity. Everything felt stuck. On a solo trip to Rishikesh, she spent hours watching the Ganges. The river didn't resist obstacles–it flowed around them.

She realized she'd been trying to control every outcome. Inspired by the river, she began practicing surrender–trusting the process, letting go of rigid plans. Her life didn't become perfect, but it became peaceful. The river taught her to move with grace, not force.

- **Neeraj, 41 – The Garden That Taught Patience** Neeraj started a small vegetable garden during the pandemic. At first, he was impatient–checking daily for sprouts, frustrated by slow growth. But nature doesn't rush. It taught him to wait, to nurture, to observe.

Months later, his garden bloomed. But more than vegetables, it gave him perspective. He began applying the same patience to his parenting, his work, and his healing. Growth, he learned, is quiet and steady–not instant.

- **Ishani, 35 – The Sky That Reflected Her Emotions** Ishani struggled with anxiety and emotional overwhelm. Her therapist suggested she spend 10 minutes each day watching the sky. At first, it felt pointless. But soon, she noticed how the sky changed–clouds came and went, storms passed, light returned.

She began to see her emotions the same way: temporary, shifting, natural. The sky became her mirror. It didn't judge–it simply held space. Nature taught her that nothing stays forever–not even pain.

"Look deep into nature, and then you will understand everything better." – *Albert Einstein*

Principle to Rise: Earth Connection: Let nature remind you of your own rhythm.

Chapter 6
Prayer as Dialogue

Prayer is often misunderstood as a one-way monologue–a list of requests, a ritual of repetition, or a desperate plea in moments of crisis. But true prayer is dialogue. It's not just speaking to the divine–it's listening. It's not just asking–it's receiving. It's a conversation between your soul and something greater, whether you call it God, the universe, spirit, or simply presence.

When prayer becomes dialogue, it shifts from performance to intimacy. It's no longer about saying the "right" words–it's about showing up honestly. You don't need perfect language. You need presence. You don't need to be holy. You need to be real.

Real-Life Examples

- **Amaan, 37 – The Conversation That Changed His Grief** After losing his mother, Amaan felt numb. He tried traditional prayers but felt disconnected. One night, he sat alone and simply spoke aloud: *"I don't know what to do. I miss you."* It wasn't scripted–it was raw.

In that moment, something shifted. He felt warmth, a sense of being heard. Over time, these nightly conversations became his healing ritual. Prayer wasn't a ceremony–it was connection. And grief became softer when he stopped trying to sound strong.

- **Lavanya, 29 – Journaling as Prayer** Lavanya didn't resonate with formal prayer. But she began journaling every morning–writing letters to the universe. She'd ask questions, express gratitude, vent frustrations. Then she'd pause and write what she felt the universe might say back.

This practice became her spiritual anchor. She didn't always get answers—but she got clarity. Prayer, for her, was a dialogue on paper. And the pages became sacred ground.

- **Ritesh, 41 – Listening in Silence** Ritesh used to pray by reciting mantras. But during a silent retreat, he was asked to sit in stillness and "listen for the divine." At first, it felt empty. But slowly, he began to notice subtle insights, emotions rising, and a deep sense of peace.

He realized that prayer wasn't just about speaking–it was about listening. The silence wasn't absence–it was presence. And in that space, he felt guided in ways words never could.

- **Nandita, 35 – Walking as Dialogue** Every evening, Nandita walked through a quiet park and spoke softly to herself. She'd say things like, "*What do I need to know today?*" or "*Show me how to let go.*" She didn't expect answers–but often, she'd feel a sudden insight or emotional release.

Her walks became her temple. Nature responded in its own way–through wind, birdsong, or a stranger's smile. Prayer wasn't confined to a room–it was woven into her steps.

"Prayer is not asking. It is a longing of the soul." – *Mahatma Gandhi*

Principle to Rise: Soulful Communication: Speak your truth. Let the divine respond in its own way.

Chapter 7
The Soul's Compass: Gut Feeling

Gut feeling is often described as a quiet inner voice, a subtle nudge that guides us when logic alone doesn't suffice. It's not some mystical force–it's a deeply practical tool rooted in our brain's ability to process information rapidly and subconsciously. When we face decisions, especially under pressure or uncertainty, our intuition draws from a vast reservoir of past experiences, emotional memories, and pattern recognition. It's our mind's way of saying, "I've seen this before," even if we can't immediately articulate why.

In real life, gut feeling shows up in countless ways. You might meet someone and instantly feel uneasy, despite their friendly demeanor. Or you're offered a job that looks perfect on paper, but something inside you hesitates. These moments aren't random–they're your brain picking up on subtle cues, body language, tone, or inconsistencies that your conscious mind hasn't yet processed. The key is learning to distinguish between intuition and impulse. Gut feeling is calm, grounded, and persistent. Impulse is loud, reactive, and often driven by fear or desire.

To use your gut wisely, you need to build a relationship with it. That means slowing down and listening. Reflect on past decisions–when did your gut steer you right, and when did you ignore it? Journaling can help you track these patterns over time. Mindfulness practices also sharpen your awareness, making it easier to hear that inner voice without the noise of anxiety or overthinking. And the more diverse your experiences, the more refined your intuition becomes. Exposure to different people, cultures, and challenges expands your internal database, giving your gut more material to work with.

Gut feeling helps by offering a rapid, instinctive form of decision-making that bypasses overanalysis and taps into your accumulated life experience. It acts as an internal warning system or green light, especially in situations where time is limited or information is incomplete. For example, when meeting someone new, your intuition might pick up on subtle cues—body language, tone, energy—that signal trustworthiness or danger before your rational mind catches up. In professional settings, it can guide you toward opportunities that align with your values or steer you away from deals that feel off, even if they look good on paper. By learning to recognize and refine this inner compass, you gain a powerful tool that complements logic and helps you navigate complex choices with greater confidence and clarity.

Ultimately, gut feeling is the soul's compass—not because it's mystical, but because it's deeply personal. It's shaped by who you are, what you've lived through, and what you value. When you learn to trust it—not blindly, but thoughtfully—it becomes one of the most reliable guides you have.

Real-Life Examples

- **Karan, 30**, felt uneasy about a job offer. He couldn't explain it—but he declined. Months later, a better opportunity arrived.
- **Rhea, 32 — Choosing Passion Over Prestige** Rhea was offered a high-paying job in a multinational firm. Everyone told her to take it—it was "the dream." But something inside her hesitated. Her soul felt pulled toward a nonprofit she'd volunteered with, even though the pay was modest.

She chose the nonprofit. Years later, she was leading impactful projects across India. Her decision didn't follow the world's compass—it followed her own. And it led her somewhere far more fulfilling.

- **Arjun, 40 – Listening to the Gut Feeling** Arjun was about to invest in a business deal that looked perfect on paper. But the night before signing, he felt uneasy. No red flags—just a quiet discomfort. He backed out, despite pressure from his peers.

Months later, the deal collapsed due to hidden liabilities. Arjun's gut had spoken—and he'd listened. His soul's compass didn't give him facts—it gave him truth.

- **Meenal, 29 – Redefining Her Identity** Meenal had always been the "responsible one" in her family. She followed every rule, met every expectation. But inside, she felt disconnected. She longed to travel, write, and explore beyond her comfort zone.

She took a sabbatical, backpacked across Southeast Asia, and started a blog. Her family didn't understand—but Meenal felt alive for the first time. Her soul's compass led her away from approval and toward authenticity.

- **Sameer, 36 – Healing Through Intuition** Kabir struggled with chronic stress and tried every conventional remedy. One day, he felt drawn to try sound healing—a practice he'd never considered. It wasn't recommended by doctors, but something inside said, "*Try it.*"

The sessions helped him release emotional blocks he didn't know he had. His healing didn't come from logic—it came from listening inward. His soul's compass guided him to what worked, even when it wasn't mainstream.

"Your heart knows the way. Run in that direction." – *Rumi*

Principle to Rise: Inner Guidance Honor your knowing—even when it defies logic.

Dear Reader,

If you've made it to this page, I want you to pause and take a breath. Not because the journey is over–but because you've come so far. You've walked through chapters that asked you to feel deeply, reflect honestly, and rise gently. That's not easy. That's brave.

This book wasn't written to fix you–because you were never broken. It was written to remind you that healing is not a straight line, and rising doesn't have to be loud. It can be quiet. It can be slow. It can be yours.

You've learned to name what hurts. To sit with discomfort. To let go of control. To trust yourself again. And maybe, just maybe, to love yourself in pieces. That's not small. That's everything.

So if you ever find yourself doubting your progress, come back to this page. Let it remind you: You are still rising. And that is enough.

With all my heart,

Yogesh Dhiman

A Final Note from the Author:

"This book was written from my heart to yours. If it helped you rise even a little, then it's done its job. Keep rising. Keep becoming. You're not alone."

You made it to the end and that means something.

Not just that you finished a book, but that you showed up for yourself. You paused, reflected, maybe cried, maybe smiled. You let yourself feel. That's not small. That's brave part of you. You're brave inside out. You're survivor, you've been survived setbacks. You're here to live on planet. One day everybody will fade away, just before that explore life. Inhale new beginings, exhale past traumas. I've done it, you can too. This is how the greatest men have lived and continue to live on this planet.